SECRET OF ESTATE SALES MARKETING SUCCESS

REAL Estate Sale Techniques & Templates To Go From Beginner To Getting An Endless Stream Of Estate Sale Clients

"Based On Selling Other People's Stuff For Fun & Profit"

By Tonza Borden

Copyright 2013 by Tonza Borden

First Edition

ISBN-13: 978-1441422453

Disclaimer: You use the information in this book and proceed at your own risk. I do not advise or instruct you to start a business. I only present appropriate educational materials to help you make an informed decision.

Users of this guide are advised to do their own due diligence when it comes to making business decisions, and all information, products and services that have been provided should be independently verified by your own qualified professionals. By reading this book, you agree that Tonza Borden and her company is not responsible for the success or failure of your business decisions relating to any information presented in this book.

Your level of success in attaining the results claimed in the instructions depends on the time you devote to the process, ideas and techniques mentioned, your finances, knowledge and various skills. Since these factors differ according to individuals, I cannot guarantee your success or income level.

Introduction

"They Laughed When I Said I'd Start My Own Estate Sale Business – But When I Got The Necessary Ingredients In Place | Started Part-Time | Achieved Profits, Success, Freedom And More They Begged Me For My Secret!"

Are you excited about starting your own estate sale business? Are you ready to understand the REAL estate sale marketing and advertising techniques liquidators have been concealing from you all these years?

You probably believe estate sale management abilities are unrelated to the beginner or do-it-yourselfer. This is not the case if you're willing to practice professional methods and operate in an established way.

Secret Of Estate Sales Marketing Success gives easy-to-follow insider recommendations and direction on how to start and manage a professional estate sale business for fun and profit. Hopefully, it will encourage you to tap into this industry to earn money by providing a problem solving service with utmost integrity.

This ebook reveals insider information and professionally formatted templates to help you develop a:

- New Client Package System with estate sale contract

- Advertising System with major estate sale promoters

- Pricing System with everyday furniture/household goods price list

- Bonus: Realtors number one key to replacing lost income in a weak housing market.

It won't happen overnight, but it's easier and **faster** than you think!

Thanks for reading this introduction. It's simply a condensed overview of a comprehensive estate sales marketing business guide.

Table of Contents

Disclaimer

Introduction

Why Almost Anyone Can Start An Estate Sale Business

Use This Micro Business Model To Do Large Estate Sales

3 Things You Need To Do To Get Estate Sale Clients To Trust You

How To Get And Satisfy Your First Estate Sale Client

How To Launch A Professional Estate Sale

How To Justify Your Estate Sale Fee In A Formula

How Is Estate Sales—Selling?

How To Set Prices To Improve Estate Sales

6 Top Techniques To Make Your Estate Sales Run Smoothly

14 Estate Sale Techniques That Will Keep You In Business

How To Write Estate Sale Policy To Warn Off Troublemakers

Why Should Estate Sale Clients Hire You - Part 1

Why Should Estate Sale Clients Hire You - Part 2

Special Bonus 1: How To Get A Steady Stream Of Estate Sale Clients With The Best Stuff To Sell

Special Bonus 2: How To Provide Cash Security For Estate Sale Clients

Special Bonus 3: How To Replace Lost Real Estate Income With An Estate Sale Business

About the Author

Estate Sale Templates

Why Almost Anyone Can Start An Estate Sale Business

If you're interested in starting an estate sale business, then look no further. Estate sales are fast becoming the next best thing in direct marketing and sales. Why? This is a business that solves a problem in the life of seniors, heirs, executors, movers and Realtors (just to name several potential clients) in a vast market that is underserved.

Not only that, the estate sale opportunity has a proven track record of integrity, honesty and quality amoung professional estate sellers and estate liquidators.

Estate sales also have longevity, not just as a service, but as a thriving industry, which comprises several related business services that facilitate this type of sales—better known as direct sales.

Does your skill set of selling, professionalism, organization, time management, personality, recordkeeping, accounting, recruiting, customer service and house cleaning items, match the requirements to be an estate seller in this booming direct sales industry?

This is the question you must ask yourself to determine whether you can do estate sales. Without some basic business skills, this book alone may prove to be more challenging than you're prepared for right now.

While you can start an estate sale business without having all of the above ingredients, it would be a lot easier if you did for the long haul. Otherwise, you may have to rely on more people to help you in those areas from the beginning. If those are your pre-existing skills, albeit a little rusty here and there, an estate sale business can very possibly become a profitable homebased enterprise for years to come.

And, here's why estate sales is a business that almost anyone can start:

- It does not take a large amount of money to start
- You become an immediate business owner
- Requires very little overhead operating from home
- You can use your present knowledge, ability and skills to work part-time or full-time
- Has almost unlimited income potential
- Promotes personal development, i.e.credibility, professionlism, etc.
- Allows you to work with who you want, when you want
- You can actually have fun while you build your business
- And more…

4 Top Questions To Answer Before Starting An Estate Sale Business

Before starting an estate sale business within the next 30 days, it is a good idea to do some basic research to answer questions about this career field. Perform Google searches for the keywords estate sale. You can also get answers about a number of important questions you'll have by reading this book as well as attending professional estate sales. Answer the following four important questions to make sure you start your estate sale business right:

1. Why do I need to use an estate sale contract?
2. What is the range of commission rates being charged?
3. How should I price items for a quick sale?
4. How do I accept payment and protect the client's money?

Use This Micro Business Model To Do Large Estate Sales

Business Model: Estate sale and estate liquidation of household goods and furnishings

Slogan or USP: "One Sale Can Help An Entire Community"

Legalities: Business license; insurance bonding, business bank account; PayPal Here™, the simple way to accept credit and debit cards, Paypal and checks—anywhere you do business, and no return policy.

Location: On-site

Commission: Percentage of total sales is charged for estate sale.

Title: Estate Seller/Estate Sale Manager

Mission: Help seniors get more money for their personal property in [Atlanta, Georgia] than they could get on their own.

Need: Most deceased individuals had too many possessions, which at the time of death must be disposed of in some manner. Most executors and heirs want to profit from the sale of their love one's personal property.

Recession-Proof: Estate sales is a senior focused business, which is based on the senior population and their needs, thus making it recession proof. Death is another part of the life cycle that isn't going to stop for a recession; and a well-run estate sale business will weather the economic storms.

Services: Estate sales, house cleaning, junk clean out/hauling

Finding Clients: The best ways to find clients is to develop relationships with estate lawyers who handle probate, and bankers who deal with trusts; retirement home managers, pastors, rabbis, charities and funeral directors:

- In charge of liquidating the personal property of an estate
- A person in the helping professions, such as professional organizers who assist others
- Someone facing life changes, such as downsizing, divorce or relocation.

Attracting Buyers: The best ways to attract professional buyers and collectors is to place ads in different collector association and society publications. Update collector's list frequently of who is buying what and where currently. Digital media channels are recommended to attract **all** types of buyers.

Basic Estate Sale Steps:

1. Conduct a free, no-obligation interview and inspection with the responsible party (prospective client).

2. Inform them to set aside personal keepsake items for the family.

3. The groundwork is put in place for a successful estate sale at this time.

4. Provide honest feed back about the options for selling items, as well as your expenses and outcomes.

5. Once the client agrees to you conducting the sale, the cleaning and sorting begins. If anything needs organizing and arranging, this is the time to do it. Advertising sells to people who are interested in what is being sold. Connect the right buyers with the products they want is the goal of this business. Advertise on estate sale promoter websites, major local newspapers (specific to sale location), Real Estate newsletter and Google Adwords.

    1) <u>Signs</u> are open to anyone who stops by. Suggested Size: 14 X 18
    2) Website with your services, contact information, preview photos and descriptions, etc. Use keywords that identify your estate sale service and specialties.

Security: It is important that your staff be available to monitor each room and answer questions.

Financial Settlement: Client must be paid at the end of the sale and presented with a complete list of items sold and not sold.

Start Up Expenses: Business license
Insurance bonding
Website and other digital media channels
New client package documents
Display tables/cases/supplies
Expenses (above items, gas...)

Sales Assistants: Spouse, friends, neighbors, etc.

Service Providers: Clean out/hauling "Broom Cleaning" services

4 Things You Need To Do
To Get Estate Sale Clients To Trust You

The first most crucial thing you need to do to get potential clients to trust you is to start a legitimate estate sale business—to avoid the label of "fly by nighter."

The second thing is to build your credibility by getting a business license through your city government, and obtain honesty bonding through an insurance company, which is necessary when managing other people's money. The third thing is to open a bank account in your business name as soon as possible.

In keeping with the above three things of building credibility, the fourth thing you need to do is collect and pay local and state taxes if applicable. All businesses are required to pay taxes (in the United States, but check with your local and state government).

These are 4 key aspects to creating a professional estate sale business that clients can check out to feel comfortable doing business with you.

Operating your estate sale business from a legal standpoint provides value to your client; and you can avoid the label of "illegitimate" or "fly by nighter."

It is beneficial and cost-effective to start as an online estate sale company; but you still need to comply with local legal requirements to run your business with integrity.

How To Get And Satisfy
Your First Estate Sale Client

Credibility is what it will take to get estate sale clients from now on. Satisfied clients will send you new clients that will keep you busy to build your business. Therefore, you must develop your credibility properly.

Because the estate sale industry is relatively new, many clients will not know exactly what you do. How you perform your services will help them to trust you. Clients will ask you exactly what you do and how you do it, and they will choose whether these are sound and trustworthy business methods.

Be ready to guide clients who may not know the estate sale process. Sometimes, they will need empathy and compassion; and this may mean taking the time to listen to what's on their mind.

Estate Sale Contract

Every client is different and has different estate sale needs so a contract is necessary that gives details about your liquidating and downsizing services, etc. Include charges for extra solutions such as packing and unpacking, housecleaning, etc. The standard cost for packing and unpacking service including boxes is $25 per person or by the hour.

When your client's needs are met, it will establish your credibility as being "service focused." Satisfied clients will deliver new clients. You will establish your credibility by having an estate sale agreement or contract, and being honest with your clients.

Be firm with more aggressive clients who insist on attending the sale and interfering with the process. The best way to handle this potential problem is to add a cancellation clause in your agreement, which gives you the option of canceling the sale should the client become aggressive, and attempt to disrupt your ability to manage the sale.

In terms of building credibility with clients and buyers, don't do pre-sales and be cautious not to let one buyer have advantage over others. Estate Sale Service Atlanta, for instance, will only do a pre-sale at a residence where public accessibility is more restricted such as a condo, gated apartment community or, private estate sale for personal reasons necessitated by the client.

Watch Out For Conflict Of Interest

Clients need your abilities, information as well as solutions. As an estate sale management service, you should not promote yourself as a buyer or concentrate on buying because it is a conflict of intention in serving them.

If managing estate sales are your main concentration, it's not okay to go on first client consultations and offer to purchase anything. Clients will ask do you buy things at the sale, to test you. This is a clear conflict of interest and can cause irreparable damage to your credibility. Decide now whether you want to be a buyer or a reputable estate seller. You cannot have it both ways.

You are responsible for your assistants who want to buy things as well. Explain to them before the sale that purchases are not allowed under any circumstances. You must maintain a strict policy of prohibiting anyone (including clients, their family and friends, assistants and yourself) from shopping before, after or during the estate sale. A clause in the estate sale agreement is usually enough to deter the client; but if you feel an overwhelming urge to ignore this policy, you should discharge yourself from estate sale management.

Your clients trust you to represent the fair and equitable sale of their personal property for their gain, not yours. You are collecting a commission based on their trust. Don't destroy your relationship or business because you or your assistants want to shop!

There may be times after the sale when beautiful things remain and the client decides to give them to you instead of donating them to a charity. In any event, do not ask for unsold household items. Charities are non-profit organizations, which means they rely on the generous donations of benevolent estate clients. Don't compete with them for these gifts.

If you have searched your mind and found no craving for these possessions, you are ready to start your estate sale business with credibility and character, which is what clients expect.

How To Launch A Professional Estate Sale

Why is it important to launch a professional estate sale? The more professional your sale is, the more success you will have. To be a good estate sale manager, it is important to have or at least develop organizational skills, which can be leveraged to build a better estate sale business.

This chapter walks you through the effective aspects of launching a professional estate sale, now and forever.

You must have the ability to see the big picture of managing an estate sale rather than getting bogged down in details. Potential problems should be anticipated, but your contingency plan should prevent them from happening. A well-organized sale, planned to the last detail, will run smoothly and help minimize the chaos that often accompanies estate sales. Planning, organizing, preparation and execution is time consuming, but the benefits pay off.

Whether you launch one estate sale or multiples, it is fun, fast-paced and you meet a lot of interesting people. However, to launch a "professional" estate sale, you need to be both strategic and technical. You need to learn and follow organized and specialized techniques of estate sale management (not a business plan per se), create a website, and use digital and social media channels to attract clients and buyers.

If you don't believe me, just check out the leading estate sale companies in your area. They are using an organized business model (strategic and technical) that has given them an edge in conducting professional estate sales, which is why they tend to charge a higher commission rate and, more for items.

You Can't Do An Estate Sale Alone

You will not be able to launch an estate sale by yourself. You will need a few other people to help you because selling and customer service are the fundamentals when it is in progress. You will be extremely busy, so your customer service assistants are important, and while being helpful to buyers, assistants must keep a watchful eye for theft and price changing. Ask your spouse, friends and relatives to help you. Once they see that you are serious and your first estate sale is successful, they will want to help you again.

You need assistants to help you with taking inventory, organizing, cleaning items, pricing, selling, customer service, i.e. collecting money, answering customer's questions, providing security, managing crowds, rearranging inventory as it sells, and other duties as assigned.

An estate sale in progress requires more eyes than hands. You will need at least two customer service assistants in a small house; or one in the basement and on each level of a large house, and two where valuables are, to protect your client's interest by preventing theft, price changing, answering questions and selling, all at the same time!

Insider Secret: The misconception about estate sales is: Nice things sell it self. Wrong! You and your customer service team have to sell them—and the easiest way is by being friendly and accommodating to buyers. Remember, that's how your new car and house was sold to you! <u>Avoid the hard sell</u>. Make sure your advertising does that with color photos and well-written descriptions.

Specialized Elements For Launching A Professional Estate Sale

From launching your first estate sale to your last, it is important to get the strategic and technical details right the first time and be consistent. Otherwise, you will lose control and every sale will become difficult. It is also important to get the visual details right the first time that makes the presentation attractive and interesting to both clients and buyers.

Your client's goal is to launch a professional and profitable estate sale. You have to produce it by exploiting the following specialized elements—to make all of your estate sales unique:

Crowd Control Number Tickets

You will need an assistant passing out number tickets, calling out numbers, and collecting tickets early in the morning, especially the first day, and while the sale is in progress. A roll of tickets can be purchased at Staples, Office Depot, etc. or you can use a deck of playing cards with handwritten numbers, or hand make and laminate your own. Just because they're handmade doesn't mean they have to look cheap. Even number tickets should represent your professionalism and attention to detail because your client will notice everything!

Not For Sale Items

During the sale, buyers poke their heads everywhere. Make sure to lock and seal off rooms with tape that you don't want buyers to enter, and post a "**DO NOT ENTER**" sign. If the client has not removed all of their personal items, heirlooms, iPods, digital cameras, and things they want to keep before the sale, make sure the client secures them in a locked room. However, the best policy is to stress to your client these things need to be removed from the home prior to the sale. In any event, make sure you address this concern in the contract stating your estate sale company will not be responsible for these items.

Checkout Area

Place a folding table near the front door for checkout, which is big enough to wrap and bag purchases. There should only be business cards, guest book and pens on it. Everything else including packaging supplies should be kept under the table. Where you keep your cashbox is entirely your business. Many estate sellers prefer to put it or the cash register on the checkout table. Give some thought to how you will make change and secure cash.

Supplies you should start buying and collecting now to be prepared for your first estate sale include:

Folding Tables

Folding tables are portable and easy to transport and setup. They are better for displaying items for sale than using furniture that's for sale. Furniture sells better when left bare so customers can appreciate its beauty and examine its craftsmanship. The same goes for cabinets, credenzas, etc. Cookware, glassware, dishes and small appliances can be arranged on countertops, and folding tables as well. Make sure tables are sturdy before displaying dishes and glassware. Cover tables with a nice tablecloth then arrange attractive displays, groupings and vignettes, which are key focal points appealing to buyers.

Carpet Runners

If you need or want to protect carpeting or flooring surfaces, be sure to lay down plastic runners and tape it so buyers won't trip. Taking this step to protect the client's property will reaffirm their decision to do business with you.

Indoor Signage

You will need several indoor signs, which will direct the flow of customer traffic and help to keep them safe. Walk through the home to determine where specific signs need to be placed such as Exit, No Exit, Garage, Downstairs, Checkout, Please Watch Your Step, etc.

Change Bank

Make sure to have a bank of at least $50-$100 for making change that consists of $1, $5, $10 and coins. Be sure to deduct your "personal money" that you use for the initial change bank on the first day, at the end of the sale. Why is this important? You should never co-mingle personal money with sale proceeds to avoid the appearance of impropriety.

Bid Box

On huge, expensive furniture, a bid box allows the client another tool to help get these items sold. A bid box works on the honor system, but can be very effective when managed correctly. For example, when several customers are interested in the same dining room set, each one is encouraged to complete a bid on a 3x5 card with their name, phone number and offer amount, and put them in a covered shoebox. Bids are usually read if the item hasn't sold on the last day of the sale, or any day you choose.

Insider Secret: Set a reserve price on high price pieces, at your client's request of course, and accept the closest offer to that figure, first come, and first served. Be careful when using this tactic, as not to set the reserve so high the item (s) remain unsold!

Price Tags

You will need extra price tags and "Sold" stickers. A key technique is using same color tags for a category of items, which will reduce price switching. For example, use green labels for furniture, yellow for accessories, etc.

Packaging

Start stockpiling (in between sales) plastic grocery bags, for small purchases and paper shopping bags for multiple items. You can never have too many because you will use them all. You will also need several small and medium size boxes to pack glassware, dishes, pottery and porcelain. Forget newsprint because it rubs off on whatever it touches. Instead, purchase tissue paper to wrap items.

Markers, Pencils, Note Pads

Keep a supply of pens, markers and notepads handy.

Tape, Small Hand Tools, Calculator

Make sure you have small and large tape dispensers for posting signs and taping boxes, etc. Small hand tools such as pliers, Phillips screwdriver and hammer can help to disassemble a piece of furniture so it can be transported easier. A working calculator just saves time even if you are a math wiz. Make sure to have one handy at the end of sale for your client's convenience to check and balance your accounting figures.

Safety And Other Considerations

Whether you have business liability insurance or not, it is a wise decision to include an agreement clause about your client's current homeowner's insurance that provides enough protection in case a buyer drops an expensive item, or injures him or herself. However, watching out for everyone's safety and posting warning signs is part of your responsibility and in the best interest of your client.

Advertising And Promotion

You will notice that estate sale advertising and promotion costs in local major newspapers exceed the price for garage sale posting, which is often free. One unique technique to reduce the cost of advertising in this media channel is to promote the estate sale in the garage sale category using all caps and bold words such as: **ESTATE SALE: EVERYTHING MUST GO or ESTATE SALE:**

SELLING OUT TO THE BARE WALLS. Make sure to promote antiques, collectibles and brand name items.

Traffic Directional Signs

You should only post estate sale directional signs where local zoning declares you can, which is a certain distance from the road. Otherwise, your expensive signs will be taken down. Not verifying with zoning authorities could cause you to be fined up to $300. Many cities are forbidding this type of sign because they are not removed after the sale, thus become litter and a community eyesore. Post these signs at the busiest street corners closest to the estate sale. It is especially beneficial if these are corners of high traffic thoroughfares during rush hour; so driver and passenger will be able to read the information (date and address). These signs can be bought at a local office supply store. If signs need to be posted on residential or commercial property, i.e. bank, go inside and ask for permission and offer your business card. Also, leave your card on the front door of private homes where you post signs when you're not able to get permission. <u>Secure it with a small piece of tape that won't leave a sticky residue.</u>

Insider Secret: Create cost-effective and eye-catching signs by typing huge, bold text on bright yellow cardstock and print several two-sided duplicates, which helps you save about $2 each. Use those two bucks to have the signs laminated and purchase 24" wood dowels (from the hardware store). The final cost for each sign is about $2, and is cheaper to substitute if some are taken down. Be sure to place these signs the day before the estate sale if possible. At the very least, place them early in the morning the first day of the sale. Most estate sales start on Friday so place the signs on Thursday evening before 5 PM (rush hour). Also, be sure to ask the homeowner to get advice from their subdivision's homeowner's association about sign placement. THIS IS CRUCIAL! If the sale is on Friday, be sure to place signs on Thursday, or no later than a few hours before rush hour on sale day. Check on your signs and replace any that are taken down.

Post Signs In Front Window And Curbside

Be sure to place a sign in the living room window; and, preferably, place an A-frame sign at the residence near the mailbox with large multi color balloons. This sign should be printed on both sides so both lanes of traffic can see it.

Preparing For Your First Estate Sale Client Call And Appointment

Before you receive your first client call, you need to be prepared for the free assessment or consultation to close the deal. Here is how you will need to respond to the phone call and what you will need to take on your first appointment:

I. "Hello. I'm Jane Doe with My Estate Sale Company. How can I help you?" or "What can I do for you?"

II. Items To Take On Your First Client Consultation:
   a. Briefcase
   b. New client folder with welcome letter, contract and other documents (See Templates)
   c. Business card
   d. Tape measure
   e. Magnifying glass
   f. Writing pad/pen
   g. Flashlight
   h. Camera/smart phone
   i. Business license/bonding copies

III. Recorded Phone Message: Thank you for calling [My Estate Sale Company!] Please state your name, phone number, and how we can assist you. Your call will be returned as soon as possible.

The client's first impression of your demeanor, business presentation and appearance is important.

Look Professional

When representing your estate sale business, you need to look professional. The standard attire of an estate seller, when going on client calls, is business casual suit, nice jacket, skirt or slacks. During the estate sale, whether your team consists of one other person or ten, make sure everyone is well dressed and well groomed if you want to make a good first impression to both clients and buyers. During the sale, your team and you can dress casual or wear company T-shirts with your logo that has a look and feel that matches your company's colors and bears its slogan (USP).

Introduction And Expert Presentation

Now that you and your business partner or assistant (for support) have introduced yourselves to the prospective client and are seated to discuss their estate sale needs and wants, and how you will be able to assist them, this is the moment you have studied, prepared and practiced pricing (on your own furniture, etc. at home) that you have anticipated. If you present yourself and documents in the client folder (briefly explaining each one and answering questions) in a professional and confident manner, your next step is to ask the client to sign the agreement. When he or she does, it will help to establish your professional credentials and burnish your "new" company's image. For more information, read chapters: *Why Should An Estate Sale Client Hire You Part 1-2.*

The Walk-Through

After chatting with your first client and getting your first estate sale agreement, you should feel more relaxed as you request to walk through the home to assess

the contents. This process is key to taking detail notes that will help you price and setup later. Having a partner or assistant there to list contents in each room, will allow you to focus on your client or taking photos.

Today, most estate sale professionals take digital photos of contents, particularly items to be featured on websites and be appraised. There's nothing stopping you from using a camcorder to produce a video tour for YouTube of valuable items that potential buyers can view.

As you are taking inventory of what is to be sold, pay close attention to each item's condition. Sometimes, the client guides the walk through so you have to be keenly observant, and be able to write fast and remember details. If the client is present; feel free to ask questions about items. This is a serious meeting—not a time for jokes or errors.

If you're a beginner, it is crucial that you ask questions related to any valuable furniture's prior written appraisals, damages, etc. You won't be able to anticipate everything to ask during this appointment, so it is perfectly acceptable to ask questions during follow-up and check-in phone calls and emails, which there will be a lot prior to the sale.

Insider Secret: Do not make any decisions until you have visited the client. Take a small bouquet of flowers because the motive is: It is a genuine gesture to build a new relationship with the potential client. Write on the card: "We value your professional relationship. Please accept this [company/corporate] gift as our genuine gesture to build a new relationship for our [estate sale or estate liquidation services]." Make sure you respond to estate sale inquiries as soon as possible to ensure your credibility and to book sales! If you don't return calls, it will leave a negative impression of your business.

How To Justify Your Estate Sale Fee In A Formula

What is the range of prices being charged to launch a "professional" estate sale? The going commission for professional estate sale service is 25%-35%. Anything less is questionable. Study the following formula for the advantages of charging a percentage fee for gross sales:

Formula Example: $5,000 (gross sales) x 25% = $1,250 + $100 (8% GA taxes if applicable) + $150 (advertising/promotion if applicable) = $1,500. Your percentage for gross sales (items sold plus city/state taxes and advertising/promotion) is $1,500.

Your client will feel the fee is worth it because of the time and hassle saved. All promotion charges and appropriate taxation must be subtracted from the total gross sales.

Sometimes, your client will want you to include the cost of advertising and promotion in the commission. This is something you need to consider and be able to respond to before it comes up.

When considering how to set your commission fee, take into account the excellence of personal property and the services engaged. Survey the amount of contents to organize, clean, display, price and advertise. The commission is more if there is a lot of work involved in these tasks for you and your team to do. Do not charge less than 25%, although some estate sale companies charge 40%-50%. I have it on good authority that some even charge 15%. I have no data as to why they feel the need to reduce the commission when the degree of effort remains the same.

Your client may insist on paying you a $1,000 minimum regardless of the sale result. If there is a lot of organizing, display, etc., the regular rate is warranted. If, during the initial assessment you see the estate has very little overall value, then you have the option to accept a $1,000 minimum or decline the sale.

Promoting "free assessments" or "free consultations" is the norm so the client must not be charged for this service. However, disposal of leftover household goods is an extra charge, or give your client the option, in the sale agreement, to dispose of it, as they want to. If there are additional costs associated with your service, make sure you tell your client before you are engaged to perform the sale. All things considered, follow the formula.

How Is Estate Sales—Selling?

When you get right down to it, estate sales means selling, which is the basis of a one-on-one relationship you must establish with your clients before the estate sale, and buyers at the point of sale.

To grow your estate sale business long-term, you must bond with clients for the duration of the sale, which is a form of selling to understand their requirements, and sell their possessions.

Can you sell? If I can do it, you, can too. There is no need for "hard selling," but merchandise in any sales environment does not sell itself. Estate sales is selling whether professional salesmanship skills are used or not.

Masters of the sales world use lighting, displays, price, beautiful women, handsome men, glossy magazine pages, etc. to enhance an items sales appeal, to sell items without virtually saying a mumbling word. That is because they know the urgency of wanting an item is greater than needing it.

The same holds true for estate sales, which is why items are arranged in attractive displays and vignettes. If you decide to become an estate seller, you will soon discover that buyers are driven by desire for things, not need for them.

Are You A Seller?

An estate seller has 2-3 days to liquidate a house full of personal property whether it's Henredon or MDF. The bigger the item, the more encouraging and persuasive you need to be in describing its usefulness to sell it, and do it with big smiles!

Everybody sells something every day. Estate sales are not just fun because of an opportunity to buy someone else's nice things for a low price; the fun atmosphere is set by the personality, friendliness, smiles, laughter and sales ability of its "sellers."

Using your personalilty will not undermine the serious nature of the sale. It will actually help you to have fun in this high stress envirnoment, and earn money at the same time. Using your personality to sell and interact with buyers is good for business.

When looking for people to build your sales team, consider retired retail managers or salesmen and women who have worked in commission based environments (professional candidates similar to retirees with SCORE). They are experienced in selling, overseeing day-to-day functions of retail sales, meeting or exceeding sales goals, sales inventory control and management, customer service, cash handling and management.

You Must Sell With Your Personality

If you have strong traffic to your estate sales but less than exciting sales, consider adjusting your personality because whether your personality is sour or outgoing, it's infectious. Make sure you are engaging, which makes a personal connection with your buyers. Your personality must be dynamic yet genuine to attract and keep buyers coming back.

When individuals, whether young or retired, are interested in being on your estate sales team, make sure you inform them about your requirement for them to engage with buyers in a friendly and accommodating manner, to facilitate the sales process. Buyers appreciate spending money in a warm and friendly atmosphere. Again, using your personalilty will not undermine the serious nature of the sale.

Inform Your Buyers—To Sell

Again, there is no need for hard selling. Provide just enough useful information about an item to persuade buyers.

Entertain Your Buyers—To Sell

Do not just sell, be entertaining. With the first fundamental of estate sales being selling, it doesn't hurt to be entertaining.

Use your people pleasing personality to entertain and sell more or all of those high-end household items, bulky items and appliances because buyers like to be entertained. If being entertaining is not your forte, then entain them indirectly:

- Entertain your buyers with music. The reason why department stores play different genres of music is to entertain shoppers because they tend to relax and spend more time in the store shopping, while enjoying the music. Loud music would be distracting, but a *Bonnie Raith* CD playing softly in the background would set the right shopping mood.

- Entertain your buyers with food. Provide a buffet for approximately 80-100 buyers with a small catering budget of $150-$200 (it's well worth it for your high-end sales – but DO NOT charge it to your client). Start the buffet after the morning sales rush on Saturday between 12 NOON -1PM. Make sure you advertise the Saturday Free Buffet with $25 minimum purchase. Let incoming buyers know that they can participate by presenting a ticket for a $25 or $50 minimum purchase. Have two assistants serviing until the food runs out. Serve two choices, i.e. fish taco and chopped BBQ sandwich, chips and ice cold soda or water and a mini pecan pie, or whatever you want. It's entertainment!

While buyers are enjoying the entertainment and fun sales atmosphere, don't forget to capture their emails in your guest book for upcoming sales.

Make sure you are providing entertainment to keep buyers buying, and anticipating your next high-end sales. In addition, make sure you discuss these entertainment ideas with your client, reassuring them no extra expense will be added to their final accounting report. Explain that providing entertainment is a complementary marketing effort solely underwritten by your company (should you choose to do it), to attract more buyers for a sell out!

Find a way to make your client's estate sale intertaining to make more profits. When the word gets around, buyers will still come to your sales for the contents, but they will stay longer and buy more because of the entertainment.

How To Set Prices To Improve Estate Sales

How can you provide value at price points both client and buyers feel is fair? Attend as many estate sales as you can to notice prices. Go to quality second hand shops, vintage shops, and auctions. Assess the prices on everything from furnishings to large appliances, making sure to take into consideration the wear and tear. Anything that is dirty, chipped, broken, torn, worn, moldy, scratched and/or cracked will not sell.

As you attend estate sales, observe the prices and take notes of what different types of things are selling for, and if you can, observe who is buying what.

Check out used furniture shops that have a reputation for selling a high volume of quality household goods, inexpensively and quickly. By analyzing their prices, you will understand what the re-sell prices are for goods in general.

It is important to note that you must do general industry research on styles and prices on a continuous basis. The industry value of items fluctuates so you must keep up with pricing of different styles. Keep in mind, just because buyers are still purchasing in a bad economy does not mean that you don't need to modify prices. The estate sale industry value of household goods is volatile, so you must keep up with changing prices.

You must be a generalist in terms of understanding a lot about many different items. Not all of your clients will have high-end furnishings. Some will have regular "everyday" and mixed match furniture and a hodge-podge of knick-knacks. Therefore, you must know industry value for similar items in different categories in regular, quality and excellent condition. Train your eye for excellence and craftsmanship.

Buy price guides on vintage furniture, antiques and collectibles, silverware, folk art, etc. Start adding these research materials to your library as soon as possible; and buy every used price guide you find in thrift stores. They may be out of print, but the descriptions will help you increase your knowledge on a broad scale. Usually, estate sale prices are estimated at about 30-60% less than what the **current** price guides list for the same item.

Insider Secret: Research your sale inventory on WorthPoint.com, which is what professional estate liquidators' use. It's faster and more convenient than comparing ads for used furniture in local newspapers. In fact, it compiles information about what various eBay items sold for.

Make sure you focus on prices that reflect the type and quality of furniture in your estate sale. If your sale is selling high-end furnishings, looking at garage sale and low-end thrift store prices will not help you. You must research the used furniture and vintage items where prices are most comparable, online or offline.

Enclosed in this e-book is a "Price List" (See Templates) that my team and I compiled and use. However, do your own research to compare the price ranges for the listed items and actual sale items. Create and continuously update your own price list to give to your assistants if you have a lot of pricing to do.

Progressively, you will become confident in pricing used furniture and vintage items and collectibles. Go to the public library and check out vintage furniture books. This is usually very beneficial and cost-effective. Watch online videos on furniture recognition and any other beneficial topics.

6 Pricing Secrets For Higher Profits

You may be wondering why pricing matters so much. When you understand the following three reasons and six pricing secrets, you will know why, which will enable you to convey the need for re-sale prices at estate sales, not retail, to your clients:

1. Set the prices too high above what people are prepared to pay, and you may end up with most of the items unsold.
2. Set the prices too low and people may perceive the items as "cheap" and lacking in quality. It is possible to have too low a price.
3. Set the prices high and then drop the price significantly after the first two hours of the sale, and your buyers may complain that they have overpaid!

So what are the pricing secrets for how to determine the right price and make a quick sale? Some of the techniques may seem a bit contradictory, but pricing is a strategy, not set in stone. If it were, there would be no after Christmas sales!

Insider Secret 1: Lowering The Prices Of High-End Items Will Increase Sales.

Estate sale buyers attend a lot of sales so they are savvy shoppers who look for and expect savings, bargains and discounts. When prices are too high, they're too close to retail markup and buyers know it! When a buyer is interested in a certain item, they do comparison pricing online first. For example: A Hancock & Moore leather sofa's asking price is $1,500. Your bottom line price is $800, but you should never disclose this price during negotiations with the buyer. Interested buyers will make an offer where they're comfortable because it is in their best interest to negotiate the lowest price possible.

Insider Secret 2: You Can Have Too Low A Price.

For example, when a high quality item is priced too low, buyers will still expect to negotiate to reduce your lowest` price. Always keep your profit margin in mind when setting prices and negotiating, and do not disclose your bottom line price. The fact that you're negotiating the item means buyers want it and you will get your price if you are patient. You have to know when to hold an item, know when to sell an item, and know when to reject an offer and walk away. The basic art of price negotiation is to let the buyer make an offer (to initiate the negotiation) because they already know your asking price. If the sofa's asking price is $1,500 and the buyer offers $500, politely say that the owner will not accept that offer. The buyer will be curious about how much the owner will accept. Keep countering their offer until you reach your bottom line price. Start mock negotiation at home!

Insider Secret 3: Pricing Above Estate Sale Competitors Won't Kill Sales.

When you post your estate sale signs, do not be surprised when sales pop up all around to take advantage of your traffic. These opportunists will drop in to check out your prices, and price their items low just to steal your buyers away because people are bargain hunters by nature. If you have done your job in advertising the sale online with photos and enticing descriptions, your buyers will come prepared to pay the cost of high quality items, which in my experience always require negotiation.

Insider Secret 4: The Best Way To Get Your Bottom Line Price Is To Let The Interested Buyer State Their Offer.

You should never let the buyer know the price that you are prepared to accept. This might sound surprising, but it is the interested buyer's responsibility to make an offer, whereby rejecting your asking price. This is a crucial technique that you must know and understand. If the buyer has made a serious offer that meets your undisclosed bottom line price or is in your price of acceptance ballpark, you can either accept it or counter. Many sellers who are new to the estate sale game, just set prices and wait for buyers to pay the asking price. That is your worst-case scenario.

Insider Secret 5: Estate Sale Buyers Don't Have A Choice; It's First Come, First Served.

Buyers are aware that to get the advertised item that they want, they have to "be" there before the sale starts, or if they have done their research already, pay for it and get a receipt immediately, before continuing to shop. Done deal! Just make sure buyers know ALL SALES ARE FINAL and NO REFUNDS!

Insider Secret 6: Prices That End In '5' or '0' Work Best.

Most estate sellers have their own method of magical pricing. We have ours too but still have to negotiate. We end our dollar amount prices in '5' or '0' because it helps us to set a better price to negotiate. For example: $7.50, $17.50, and $345—you get the idea. It may only be psychological, but we don't lose anything by using it and buyers don't object to it.

6 Top Techniques
To Make Your Estate Sales Run Smoothly

What makes estate sales run smoothly? There are many important parts in the estate sale machine, and each one can be implemented in specific ways, but there are 6 top techniques that require intense study and concentration to make your estate sales run smoothly.

Organization

Organize and display room by room. For example, kitchenware and glassware should be displayed in the kitchen. Furniture should be set up in "show room" style. Leave clothes hanging in closets. Exercise equipment and seasonal decorations can be organized on shelving (if available) and/or on basement, garage, porch, deck and patio floors.

Informal Appraisal

Informal appraisal is your opinion of the value of personal property, which is one of the most challenging tasks. If there are valuable antiques and collectibles, it is crucial to seek the services of a certified appraiser. For informal appraisal intents and purposes, estate sellers render opinion of value to set prices based on condition, research and comparison. This technique becomes more accurate with experience and research.

Pricing

Pricing personal property can also be challenging. Your goal is to price each item for a "quick sale" and generate cash. It is interesting to note that personal property is only worth its price tag if a buyer is willing to pay it. No prices should be set in stone or retail markup. Negotiate, negotiate, and negotiate! The same goes for regular furnishings and appliances. Price it for a quick sale and it will be a win, win situation for everyone!

Timing

Setting a date for the estate sale is another key strategy for estate sales to run smoothly. Weather is an important factor to consider in different regions. For example, if you host an estate sale in the dead of winter in Atlanta, Georgia, very few people will attend. However, it is the opposite in northern USA. Understanding your geographical markets will help you determine the best times to launch sales for a higher number of buyers.

Advertising And Promotion

All of the above-mentioned techniques are crucial for estate sales to run smoothly, but advertising and promotion is the key to attracting buyers. After your client has selected sale dates that give you at least two weeks lead-time, create and publish ads in the local major newspaper (specific to where the sale is located), and on all major and small estate sale websites on the Internet. If you have created a client package including advertising plan, etc, you should be hitting the ground running!

Deploy these 6 top techniques to your planning and execution strategy to make your estate sales run smoothly. Combined with your confidence, perseverance, and a lot of targeted effort, they will run like a well-oiled machine!

14 Estate Sale Techniques
That Will Keep You In Business

1. Negotiation

You will get counter offers from the beginning of the estate sale. As the manager who has done the pricing, and who possesses the most knowledge on the various items for sale, you have the authority to accept or refuse offers. As a representative of your client, you are personally invested in the sale, therefore, must make the hard decisions of selling items, and reducing prices. Remember, drastic reductions should not be made at the beginning of the sale unless an item was overpriced by mistake or is damaged. Adjust prices early in the sale only if there is low in-coming traffic and/or lack of interest in certain large items.

You should not hesitate to consider any offers during negotiation, but you are not obligated to accept any either. Be prepared to reject offers for items combined in a set. For example, a buyer makes an offer for the only night stand in a bedroom set. If you sell any item from a set, you have decreased its re-sale value, and the set may not sell.

2. Cleaning

If possible, clean items. Glasses, pots, and even bedspreads sell faster if they are clean and do not smell. Use Oxiclean on chenille bedspreads that have been in storage. This product removes the yellowing that occurs on fine white linens as well. Dishes and glassware should all be spotless. Unless its fine stemware, wash them in the dishwasher. Dirt decreases value of any item. Ask the homeowner to spruce up the floors, counters and clean out the refrigerator—for sale or not. Cleaning is a good reason to improve the sales environment.

3. Parking Logistics

Notify the Police and remind your client to notify the subdivision homeowners association of the sale. This is important in communities where parking is a problem. Some city ordinances may require alternate parking for estate sales. Informing the Police of the sale will prevent parking tickets on buyers vehicles. Make sure you assertively remind buyers not to block driveways or park on sidewalks. Consider adding this to your policy.

4. Display

Besides tablecloths, tables and furniture pieces to display items as necessary, portable racks are useful as well. Large quantities of regular scarves, lingerie, gloves, etc. can be sold in separate uncovered boxes if space is limited and post a sign: $1 each.

5. Organization

Organize and display room by room. For example, kitchenware and glassware should be displayed in the kitchen. Furniture should be set up in "show room" style. Leave clothes hanging in closets. Exercise equipment and seasonal decorations can be organized on shelving (if available) and/or on basement, garage, porch, deck and patio floors.

6. Guestbook

Make sure your assistants encourage new buyers, previous buyers and loyal buyers to sign the Guestbook to be notified of upcoming estate sales. Buyer's contact information changes so remind them to sign the Guestbook to update it as well. This is crucial to build a following to your sales.

7. Contract

If family members have not had a chance to retrieve heirlooms and items that they want, and your client and you are in agreement, arrange for them to remove the items before the sale. List them in the contract as "items not to be sold." If your client decides to remove items after signing the contract, do not hesitate to refer him or her back to the agreement clause about removing things from the estate sale after the contract has been signed. Make sure this transaction is clearly annotated in the contract, which includes asking prices because this reduction in inventory may negatively impact gross sales.

8. Manpower

You cannot do a sale alone. Assistants and helpers should arrive at least one hour early to get organized, and get instructions from you to make any last minute adjustments.

9. Policy

Some buyers will attempt to gain access to the sale earlier than publicized. They're called "early birds." Pickers, collectors and antique dealers want to be the first ones in, and may use ploys. Do not give preferential treatment to anyone under any circumstances to protect your credibility.

10. Online Advertising

Advertise and promote large pieces prominently in online advertising, i.e. antiques, large furniture, washer and dryer.... EstateSales.org estate sale posting fee includes an ad on Craigslist, which is a feature I love. For best online advertising results, use the major paid estate sale promoters: EstateSales.net, EstateSales.org, TagSellIt.com, and GAEstateSaleNetwork.com.

11. Pricing

Pricing is the most difficult part of the estate sale. If it weren't, all sales would sell out! Unlike auctions that offer the opportunity of potentially realizing the full retail value of a particular item or exceeding it; pricing for an estate sale requires knowledge of many types of items, and informal opinion of the highest price the market will bear. Adjust prices for low in-coming traffic or lack of interest in large items. You should not promise your client more than you can deliver. Being overly optimistic about pricing does disservice to your client—and your business.

12. Reference Books

Buy books on antiques, collectibles, furniture, etc. to use as a guide in pricing items and to learn the descriptions. Beginners should start to use online references to research such as WorthPoint.com until it becomes second nature.

13. Safety

Walk through the entire house to identify any obstacles that might be a safety hazard for anyone. Identify the traffic patterns and post "safety" signs as needed. If the house is wheelchair accessible or not, note that in your advertising.

14. Disposal

If your estate sale doesn't sell out to the bare walls, inevitably there will be unsold items. There are several cost effective ways of disposal. Not for profit stores or homeless shelters will accept most items except broken appliances or used mattresses. Donated items are tax deductible; but your clients must receive an itemized receipt with dollar amount. If there is an enormous amount of inventory leftover, most charitable organizations have pick up service. Be sure to schedule ahead and ask what items they will not accept.

Or, haul the items near the curb and label it with a "free sign." This disposal method may take too long and a lot of items will remain curbside causing a community eyesore. Call a cleanout and hauling service to pickup free leftovers that are saleable, in lieu of payment. Last by not least, charge the client to have a Bagster® (dumpster in a bag) dropped off and picked up on a scheduled date.

How To Write Estate Sale Policy To Warn Off Troublemakers

This estate sale policy may sound matter-of-fact, off-putting and downright rude to some potential buyers, but they are necessary to let people with disruptive intentions know that you take your client's estate sale seriously, and will not tolerate disruptive behavior.

By now, you should already know what a professional estate sale is, how it works, and what its successful and profitable results mean to your client, and your business.

An estate sale is typically much more professional and eventful than a garage sale or yard sale, so there is much more riding on its outcome.

The public is invited into the home and given the opportunity to purchase any item that is priced for sale. Unfortunately, there is no way to determine what intentions people have in mind, which could be disruptive to your sale. Therefore, it is crucial to post a strong estate sale policy on the front door that starts with the following statement:

<u>LAST MINUTE WARNING:</u> We only want to have positive-minded people at our estate sale. If you like to push, shove, complain or think people owe you their precious time, then please do NOT enter. There are other estate sales out there that will be happy to "serve" you...

Estate Sale Policy

- No Early Birds Allowed.

- Pricing Info Will Not Be Given Out Prior To Sale.

- Buyer Is Responsible For The Removal Of Items Once Purchased. Pick Up Times Cannot Be Arranged At A Later Date.

- Entry To Home May Be Limited For Security Reasons.

- Use The Website To Read Sale Descriptions.

- Cash Only. Bring Small Bills.

- We Will Not Accept Worn, Torn, Faded, And Any Defaced Bills. **The Bank Will Not Accept Them Either**.

- We Well Not Make Change For $20 Denomination And Up For Small ($1) purchases. No Exception.

- Do Not Block Driveways Or Park On Sidewalks. If You Do The Police Will Give You A Ticket.

- Be Considerate Of Your Fellow Shoppers. <u>Police Will Be Called To Settle Disputes.</u>

- Examine Items Closely And Carefully Before You Pay For Them.

- First Come, First Served. Leaving The Property Means You Have Abandoned Your Place In Line.

- If Price Tag Is Removed Or Switched, Prices Will Be Re-assigned At Checkout.

- Hoarding Is Not Allowed! You Must Buy What You Pile Or <u>Will Be Asked To Leave</u>.

- NO STROLLERS. It Is Not A Good Idea To Bring Children To Sales. If An Item Is Broken You Pay For It.

- Please Try To Leave Your Large Purse Or Bag At Home When Attending Sale.

- All Items Must Be Removed Day Of Sale--No Loading Assistance Provided.

- Items Sold AS IS, NO REFUNDS, NO EXCHANGES, NO RETURNS, ALL SALES FINAL.

- Any Items Paid For But Not Picked Up By [Sale Date] Will Be Donated.

Why Should Estate Sale Clients Hire You - Part 1

Estate sales may look easy from the outside, but they are not. As an estate sale novice, do not agree to do your client's estate sale with the intention of hastily throwing it together as an "indoor garage sale." A professional estate sale requires forethought, planning and confidence to deliver results—success and profit. And, clients expect you to be present and accountable, at their sale!

This article will cover important components of the estate sale you should discuss with the client to reassure them that you are a professional and can relieve them of hard work and hassle of launching the sale. Remember to point out the difference between an estate sale and garage sale is hiring a professional (you) to provide effective advertising, pricing, security and organization.

Estate sales can actually be very frustrating and can take a toll on you psychologically. They are not just for managing the personal property of a deceased person, but can be used to downsize when a mother or father transitions to an assisted-living facility, hospice, etc. Why should these clients consider choosing your estate sale company to deal with their family member's estate dispersal?

If a client is confused and basically doesn't know where to begin, contacting a professional estate liquidation company is supposed to reduce the emotional strain, and time it takes to put on an estate sale—not add to it.

Estate liquidation professionals help clients make the hard personal choices such as what to keep, what to sell, and what to donate.

Discuss Organization

During the new client interview and preliminary assessment of personal property, you must take the lead to inform them about what they are responsible for removing and/or securing, in terms of heirlooms they want to keep or give to a specific family member or charitable organization, prior to the sale. Generally, after the sale inventory, the **estate sale contract** will prevent your client from removing personal property after the agreement has been signed.

Initially, potential clients don't know why they should hire you. It is your responsibility to articulate the following reasons to them why they should:

- Estate sale liquidators can better determine asking prices for sale items because of your expert knowledge, and reference materials to assist you in pricing items.
- Estate sale liquidators must be licensed and bonded when handling someone else's money and you have these credentials.

The New Client Interview Is Not Guaranteed Acceptance

During the new client consultation or assessment, you should be prepared to be interviewed, and offer a ballpark estimate of what the sale could net, when asked. Potential clients may test your price confidence by asking you to price a few valuable items or the entire inventory. Inform them that you need more time to research and prepare a written report with items and estimated selling prices; but it will not be a formal appraisal, if you choose to do it.

Make sure you clearly explain your company's estate sale contract in terms your client can understand; that states your commission fee and additional costs for services such as housecleaning, etc.

Some estate sales are performed on the $1,000 minimum basis and not a percentage of sales. Your client may insist on paying the $1000 minimum in anticipation of a low grossing sale.

Whether the sale earns $2,000 or $5,000, your estate sale company will be paid the minimum. Standard percentage rates for estate sales range from 25% to 40%. Some estate liquidators have been known to charge as low as 15% per sale; but I have no data as to why they feel the need to reduce the commission when the degree of effort remains the same. Are you prepared to address the $1,000 minimum and what your company's commission is?

Services delivered by your estate sale company should consist of advertising, pricing, security and organization (among other components), which includes after sale responsibilities and "broom cleaning" the property to leave it free of unsold items and boxes. If your client's estate sale involves additional services and have extra expenses connected to it, make sure they are detailed in the contract.

Discuss Organization And Security

Be prepared to state that you are capable of arranging items neatly and attractively in their respective spaces, and you are creative in using displays and table covers for showing off items. Reassure your client that their valuable sale items will be displayed in secure portable glass display cabinets and under strict security controls.

Why Should Estate Sale Clients Hire You - Part 2

In some cases, the family of a deceased family member may be able to handle an estate sale—in a garage sale manner. However, for the greatest amount of profit, a professional estate sale is the best choice if the house contains an enormous amount of quality items. This is an important concern to your client so your estate sale knowledge, experience and confidence may be questioned.

Again, take the lead; estate sale clients need your guidance and expertise. That is why they chose to contact you. Informing them "NOT to throw anything away" may sound trivial but one man's junk can be sold for a dollar here and a dollar there, which can increase gross sales. Advise them not to sell items hastily and cheaply at a garage sale or yard sale, have a do-it-yourself estate sale, or consign to an auction, but to let "your" estate sale company be the judge. They will be impressed by your knowledge and dedication to take profit.

Answering client's tough questions during the new client interview honestly and confidently is the right thing to do. Present your knowledge, experience and confidence in a professional manner.

If you are just starting your estate sale business and doing sales part-time, how will you address the question, "Do you do sales on a regular basis?" Some estate liquidation experts recommend that clients not hire a company that doesn't do sales on a regular basis.

I have been a professional estate liquidator for over 14 years, and at times it is necessary to limit bookings, as my company did temporarily, so I could write this book, which answers the request of many individuals for information about becoming an estate sale professional. In so doing, we are scheduling 6-12 sales a year, and recommending other professional estate sale companies.

The point is, if you are a new estate sale company; do not be afraid to answer questions about your part-time booking schedule. Let clients know you are interested in building your business, and appreciate the opportunity of meeting with them for the possibility of managing their estate sale.

Usually, clients have already accepted you to launch their sale before they contact you. They have visited your website, and taken the time to read through it, which answered basic questions about your services, and testimonials, which is a key indication of your credibility. If they are informed consumers with digital media access, they have probably contacted the Better Business Bureau for complaints about your company as well.

As I am taking on the role of sharing estate liquidation information with individuals who want to become a professional estate seller; I also advocate that an estate sale novice should not be automatically labeled a "fly by nighter," simply because he or she is a beginner and/or don't have regular bookings. I feel very fortunate for former clients who gave me a chance in the beginning, and every new client who still does.

Every professional estate seller is not listed on Angie's List, nor do beginners have word-of-mouth recommendation. That is why I am providing information for beginners to make an informed decision to start and operate a professional estate sale business—to earn acceptance and business references.

Discuss Advertising

Will your advertising attract buyers that clients will see lined up at the house on every sale day?

Inform your client you need at least three weeks lead time before the sale to advertise and stoke buyer's desire for certain items. Ads should be placed on major estate sale promoter websites and in local major and community newspapers for a full two weeks prior to the sale (this is crucial).

If you are more interested in booking back-to-back sales, you will not have time to do effective advertising and promotion. One major online estate sale promoter, EstateSales.org, includes advertising on Craigslist, which attracts a lot of viewers. Set an advertising budget for each sale and manage it to target a specific estate sale market. For example, if your sale is in Kennesaw, Georgia, target the major newspaper for that area first!

These ads typically cost $50 including bold headline and 5 lines of text, which is adequate; just state who, what, when and where in the ad. Frequent estate sale buyers' check for sales every week so make your ads stand out by listing antiques, collectibles, tools, brand names, etc.

If your advertising isn't executed according to an Advertising Plan (see Templates), within two weeks lead-time from the actual sale date, your sale may fail. <u>Advertising buys traffic and traffic generates sales.</u> You need a written advertising plan at minimum to know how to get traffic, where to get traffic and when your traffic (buyers) will see your ads. Personally, I budget $150 to advertise each estate sale and the sample Advertising Plan (See Templates) shows how I itemize it. The only thing that changes is local newspaper(s) in the vicinity of the estate sale.

An effective advertising strategy should include classified ads in newspapers, on the Internet, signs, and fliers, with color photos and detail description of items for sale, dates of sale and policy. At the end of the sale, the client reimburses the $150 advertising cost, itemized on the final accounting summary.

Signs are crucial to your advertising strategy to attract and bring buyers to your sale. Your signs must also compete with other signs, so make them stand out! They don't have to be the biggest and boldest, but nice and to the point—because they represent your client and your company.

Many estate sellers neglect sign appearance, which is why you see dinky estate sale signs with no directional arrows. Depending on your budget, there are a couple of ways to have professional signs printed.

1. Have a sign shop print them with "ESTATE SALE", dates, address and directions.
2. Create the signs yourself and have them laminated, which are the most cost effective.

The day before the sale and before rush hour, post the signs in a five-mile radius to the house, and on the corner of busy intersections.

Discuss Pricing

The pricing component is what will prompt your client to ask, "What happens to things that don't sell?" Remember: They are only interested in selling out to the bare walls. To achieve this goal, express to them that setting unrealistic, retail or expensive prices will result in fewer sales and unsold items at the end of the sale. Let them know that you will work hard to price even the smallest items (without giving it a garage sale atmosphere). Your goal is to price everything at the right price for a "quick sale," which will ensure fewer disposals after the sale and more importantly larger gross sales.

The last thoughts on why an estate sale client should hire you is: Before accepting the estate sale, make sure you provide a detail, professionally written contract spelling out exactly what your client and you get for your hard work.

Discuss After Sale Responsibilities—Final Accounting Summary

Make sure you inform your client that you will prepare an itemized accounting summary that includes gross sales, commission fee, services, advertising (if the client is reimbursing this cost), and net amount payable to your company, and the net amount payable to them. Donated items and their value should be listed on the donations form made out to the client. Skip this step if your business is not a non-profit.

Again, let your client know how often you do estate sales. Let them know the reasons you don't stay busy, i.e. you're retired and work part-time, or you're a Realtor or interior designer who has transitioned to estate sales with an extensive list of potential buyers... Just answer the client's questions and offer information that is pertinent to sealing the deal.

Would you feel comfortable and capable if your potential client visited one of your sales before signing the contract? This could happen and is an excellent way for them to develop a true impression of how you will manage their estate sale.

Advertising, pricing, security and organization, in addition to research and professionalism, are the keys to launching and managing professional estate sales. If your prospective client visits one of your sales and observe your inability to manage and a disorganized environment, they will dismiss you from consideration. When they observe you taking charge with staff, selling and engaging buyers, and all rooms are organized and items clearly tagged, they will be impressed and moved to offer you their estate sale.

At the conclusion of your first client interview, ask for final questions. If there aren't any, remind your client that you have included a list of frequently asked questions with answers about your company's services in their client package; and graciously thank them for their time—and hopefully their estate sale!

You should do your best to be a true professional estate seller. In so doing, you will get hired by estate sale clients, get business referrals, and establish a following of loyal buyers to your estate sales!

Bonus 1: How To Provide Estate Sale Cash Security For Clients, Buyers And You

Money is the essence of estate liquidation and a huge responsibility for the estate seller. It is also a very sensitive subject. The following tips will help you to provide cash security and theft prevention for your clients, buyers and you at your estate sales.

As an estate seller, you are in control of the estate sale cash and should have an understanding of cash collection supported by receipts and/or cash register tape, and security. Cash handling requires control measures that must be monitored continually, by you, to detect any markdown theft, price switching, shoplifting and/or cash skimming. Any one of these security breaches can result in a substantial loss to your client.

Markdown

Only the estate seller should be responsible for reducing prices to make a sale. A great deal of money may be lost if each one of your assistants is not keeping track of asking price and selling price. They should each have an Itemized Sales List (See Templates) attached to a clipboard to list items as they are sold, and give you the correct dollar amount for each sale. Take time to count what they give you; don't just take their word for it—no matter how busy you are.

When cash is transferred from an assistant to you or from buyer to you, it should be counted in the presence of both parties. The amount should be recorded on your Itemized Sales List or at least log each one of your sales. This is necessary for the purposes of establishing responsibility for shortages. Cash shortages must be reported on the Financial Accounting Summary (See Templates) and deducted from your commission payment.

Price Switching

If your estate sale lasts two or three days, wait until the last day to mark things down drastically. Before the sale, walk through several times to make sure everything is tagged securely. Make sure each assistant has an Itemized Sales List (inventory) with pricing to cross check for price changing, etc, because it is impossible to remember all of the prices. Beware of buyers switching prices on expensive items with too low a price tag and/or palming small items. Theft by price switching and covert theft is always an issue.

Shop Lifting And Cash Skimming

When cash is transferred from buyers and assistants to you, it should be counted in the presence of both parties. Any amount of money that is transferred between buyers, assistants and you is a "big deal" because you have a fiduciary responsibility to protect your client's money, i.e. by hiring a licensed security guard, an off duty policeman and/or taking other precautions.
Other precautions include using the front entrance as the exit, and assigning one person in each room of the house to watch anyone with large purses or coats continuously. Do not keep large sums of money available for temptation. Make repeated trips to the bank if necessary with security escort. Develop your own cash control plan, as this is entirely your business.

Choose people to work with very carefully. They need to be trustworthy; and make sure they are held accountable for their actions and behavior. Write an estate sale agreement for your assistants to sign and date that holds them accountable. If you do decide on a professional estate sale career, you should check your helpers out thoroughly. Get references from previous estate sale employers.

Top Estate Sale Cash Handling Tips

- Do not use a cash box for obvious reasons. Wear a waist pack or waitress apron.

- Secure the proceeds and anything related to cash control.

- Do not accept checks or credit cards—that may be stolen—and charge backs aren't worth the time and effort.

- Beware of counterfeit bills. Mark bills from $20 denomination and up with a counterfeit pen/marker that you can buy at office supply stores.

- Do not accept worn, torn, faded and any defaced bills. **The bank will not accept them either.** It might be all the buyer has, but do not accept it. If you do cash only sales, make sure you post this in your policy.

- Do not make change for $20 denomination and up for small purchases. This is a common practice of counterfeiters. Post this in your policy as well. Don't worry about offending a few buyers. Be tactful as possible, but you are accountable to your client!

Proper Change Making Procedures

When someone hands you a bill to make a purchase, leave the bill out in view until you've given him or her change. This will help clear up any misunderstanding when they claim they gave you a larger bill.

After you have tendered change, put a "change sticker" on his or her change, and place a change sticker by the item they purchased on the Itemized Sales List or sales log. This way, if they come back to 'query' the change you gave them; you can show them your change sticker. For example, they gave you $20 to pay for a $5 item. You gave them $15 change with a change sticker, and write $20/15 on both stickers. If you can think of a better way do it.

Speak the transaction like sales clerks do. For example, say whatever the price is (or after markdown), "The price is $20 and you gave me $50 so I owe you $30, right?" Always count the money so both parties can see it is the correct change.

Do not keep a large wad of cash on you. Take care of estate sale business, as you need too. Keep a change bank of up to $100 only.

I don't want to conclude this article without pointing out a few tips for buyers to protect their money from pickpockets.

Pick Pocketing

Watch your purse, wallet and back when you are at estate sales (or any public place) because pick-pocketing experts could be anywhere trying to steal your cash, credit cards and identification. Take the following precautions to secure your personal valuables when shopping:

- Men, put a rubber band around your wallet. Supposedly, that makes it harder to slide out.
- Men, get a money belt and/or wear the old-fashioned button front shirts.
- Ladies, carry your long strap shoulder bag around your neck. This way you will know where it is at all times. Remember to not keep all your eggs in one basket!
- Stay alert to people getting too close for comfort.

Bonus 2: How To Get A Steady Stream Of Estate Sale Clients With The Best Stuff To Sell

Who Are The Potential Clients For Your Estate Sale Business With The Best Personal Property To Sell?

For the most part, seniors have accumulated the most and best personal property over the years, especially since the Great Depression. A period when they had to make do with what they had and could not afford to throwaway anything, which caused many of them to hang on to things until they have to move or forced to downsize. Then the question becomes what can I take with me? Downsizing produces new possessions for estate sales that were unavailable.

People in general have things that they acquire in order to explore a new hobby, not to mention obsolete fashions, footwear and house wares. Downsizing is usually necessitated by involuntary circumstances such as illness, death of a spouse, move-in with children or into a small apartment, divorce or relocation. Whatever the reason, the process of de-cluttering, purging, thinning, sorting or disposing has begun to downsize a home filled from top to bottom with acquisitions spanning one's lifetime, marriage, etc. Throughout one's life, young or old, people typically accumulate a large volume of personal property.

The best personal property to sell is also accumulated from businesses and other family members, growing larger as time passes. Disposing of possessions occurs in conjunction with downsizing, which in many cases will only allow people to acquire new things.

Why Are Seniors Potential Clients With The Best Personal Property?

Seniors typically have accumulated a massive amount of things for different reasons, i.e. out of necessity, as gifts, or any one of the following reasons:

- Things are useful and help them in one-way or another.
- Things are worth something so they hold onto them because they could never recoup the value or what they paid for them.
- Things satisfy and seem to fulfill a purpose for keeping them.
- Things represent them in terms of vocation, hobby, travels, and volunteer work.
- Things represent a time capsule in that it is hard to give up things that conjure the past or the future. For instance, I maintain an antiques room that reminds me of my grandmother's house, and quilt squares that I plan to make quilts from…someday.
- Things for giving because it makes them feel good to share, knowing that their things will help someone else.
- Things that represent family heirlooms that can be passed down to future generations to continue the family history.

- Things not wasted prevent want of useful things and seniors can remember the hardships of the Great Depression and how difficult it was to throwaway useful things.

As there are various reasons why seniors acquire and keep things, there are just as many problems associated with downsizing and dispersal of things. Not only must they address the living space of a family home, but also the attic, basement, garage and storage areas.

Not only are seniors potential clients with the best household goods, they are also faced with a difficult task of establishing housekeeping in a new, smaller space and the daunting task of rearranging their belongings to fit the space, and whom can they enlist to help them.

What Are Some Of The Little Known Ways Estate Liquidators Can Find These Potential Clients?

Estate sale companies that host frequent sales with quality personal property, consistently take advantage of these little known techniques to get potential clients with the best household goods to sell, which are:

- Posting invitations to host sales in senior high-rise building communities, and in a senior community newspaper
- Going to the courthouse to look up public records for probate filings, and mailing a standard introductory letter to the estate executor of the will. Real Estate agents are already aware of this strategy, but most estate sellers are unaware of this great tactic.
- Contacting the family before the death becomes public record (if possible) by establishing a working relationship with the funeral home.
- Becoming an established estate sale service resource in your church.

How To Identify Potential Clients With The Best Personal Property To Sell?

All of your initial and future estate sale planning and marketing should revolve around getting clients, so it's crucial that you know who your potential clients are.

Work through the following checklist to determine just whom they are that you should be focusing on to market your estate sale business and sell the best personal property:

- Are your clients moving to an assisted living facility?
- Are your clients downsizing from a large home?
- Are your clients selling a home?
- Have your clients lost a loved one?
- Are your clients divorcing?
- Are your clients relocating?
- Are your clients pending foreclosure?

- Are your client's heirs, executors or personal representatives?

The more you know about who your clients are and where they are, the better you can serve their estate sale needs and solve their problem.

How Will You Market To Your Potential Clients?

Here's a short list of marketing mediums that estate sale liquidators and professionals use to reach potential clients:

- Direct sales letter with brochure and business card
- Email sales letter with electronic business card
- Website
- Realtors, probate lawyers, churches, funeral homes, assisted living facilities, etc.
- Google Adwords and search engine marketing
- Social networks such as Facebook and LinkedIn
- Video-sharing sites such as YouTube and its competitors.

You need to work through the above components before starting your estate sale business.

This is a simple approach to getting a steady stream of estate sale clients with the best personal property to sell, if your message is compelling enough to attract them away from the competitors.

Bonus 3: How To Replace Lost Real Estate Income With An Estate Sale Business

The housing market went over the cliff several years ago and took the lucrative incomes of many of its Realtors with it. While some have simply walked away from their shattered dream career, others are holding on until it makes a full recovery. This article is not for those who have money and time to wait it out, but for those who didn't have a back-up income plan, but now aspire to start an estate sale business. With that goal, it is to your advantage to learn how to serve clients simultaneously as a Realtor/Estate Sale Agent.

In view of the current housing situation, it is a buyers market and an estate liquidation market as well. When a house is for sale in addition to needing possessions liquidated, a Realtor/Estate Sale Agent can increase its exposure, and organize the estate sale to its best advantage, which all buyers will see, talk about, and buy the contents.

Being a Realtor/Estate Sale Agent requires specialized knowledge including license to sell real property. Some of you may have formal appraisal or informal appraisal skills, which can quickly and easily translate into an estate sale business. Some Realtors are now making a lucrative income by transferring their experience to the estate sale market; because you can start out with no estate sale experience and host your first sale in next to no time. Basically, all it takes is this guide, your confidence, and motivation to work hard. You will soon have the ability to launch and control everything about the estate sale such as:

- Room and display arrangements
- Advertising
- Sales negotiation
- Security
- Pricing
- Recruiting assistants for selling, crowd control, etc.
- Disposal of unsold items

Realtor/Estate Sale Agent Benefits

- Estate sale can take place in the house that's for sale
- Everything can be sold individually, which creates larger income
- You are a dual professional
- Commissions are usually higher (25%-30%)
- Because estate sales take place over 2-3 days, more buyers can attend
- Prices are set and all items are marked
- Targeted and effective advertising
- Social and digital media channels to inform your network about the home and estate sale.

Why are estate sales Realtors number one key to replacing lost Real Estate income? The fact that you are already established in business, and have an extensive referrals' list means you are two thirds closer to estate sale success and income replacement. You are the master at working a referrals' list and directing sales letters to target property sellers and professionals. Successful estate sales for you are in your referral's list, but your commission income is in the traffic to your sales.

To get the right kind of estate sale clients, use an existing Real Estate referrals' list or build one if you are a novice in both arenas. This technique is so powerful; it can take you from zero sales in Real Estate to becoming a powerhouse Realtor/Estate Sale Agent, faster than you think!

4 Key Benefits You Can Provide Your Estate Sale/Real Estate Clients

- Most of the time the deceased loved one left behind many items of value, which are split between the heirs. You can liquidate the valuable and less valuable items for fast cash.
- You can help take the burden off your client's shoulders so they can get on with their life.
- You specialize in selling leftover personal property from deceased estates. You will organize and sell it, as is, without repairs or moving any items in the estate.
- Another key to your success is to always ask potential clients, "Do you need to sell the personal property fast? If yes, you can assist them.

As a dual professional, you will host estate sales from the homes that may also be for sale; and do your best to make the process as simple and hassle free as possible, while replacing your lost Real Estate income.

Insider Secret: Explain to the funeral director that you want to help families settle their estates by selling their personal property, and selling their Real Estate after probate is complete.

Select a sympathy card and write: I am sorry for your loss. I know this is a very difficult time for your family; and I sympathize with you in your time of grief. I want to introduce myself and let you know I can help when you are ready to settle your Estate in the upcoming months. I manage Estate Sales and can liquidate your personal property, i.e. furniture, house wares, automobile (with title), etc. in as little as 2-3 days. Please contact me when you are ready to discuss it. We care.

Ask the funeral director to put your business card with the family's care package that they'll receive from the funeral home. Don't expect an immediate response. Grief is a lengthy process so it may take as long as a year or more before you receive a response. When it's time for them to pay bills for the estate (utilities, taxes, lawn care, etc.) they will see the need for an estate sale and sale of the house.

Estate sale client's option to hire you to launch their estate sale or to sell their home creates the following benefits and challenges:

- Challenge: Real Estate and estate sales have gone digital so a percentage of your business income is in Internet marketing. It is important to understand the different ways that both types of clients, and homebuyers and estate sale buyers can view advertising to search for liquidation companies, Realtors, estate sales, and dream homes.

- Benefit: A Realtor takes 6% commission off the selling price of the home.

- Benefit: Becoming a Realtor/Estate Sale Agent means you can take from 25% to 40% off the gross estate sales (in addition to the Real Estate commission), and do the Internet marketing for both sales. When potential estate sale clients interview you, make sure they know about your ability to do dual marketing of their personal property and home.

- Challenge: If you are not familiar with digital media channels such as Internet marketing (website), social networking and instant mobile media, you are doing your clients and your business a disservice. You need to seriously consider creating a website as soon as possible. Advertising, promotion and marketing has evolved from placing ads in newspapers. The world has gone digital and you need to become a Realtor/Estate Sale Agent that understands new marketing media channels. Estate sales are sold with Internet marketing, yard signs, newspaper ads, flyers and word of mouth. Real Estate must be promoted online in a dozen different ways—and not just Facebook!

- Challenge: Launching estate sales for potential clients who are also selling their homes can be a tricky process. You need to be able to meet with them on-site, according to their schedule; and you must be able to answer tough questions about estate liquidation.

- Benefit: Being able to function as a Realtor/Estate Sale Agent is why potential clients will choose you over regular estate sale professionals to launch their sale and sell their home.

The new client interview/consultation/assessment is not the time to discuss selling the house—unless your client brings it up. However, during the walkthrough, take mental notes about areas that need to be updated with paint, flooring, fixtures and lighting, etc. If the house is in good condition, but they haven't updated the faucet in the sinks, the doorknobs, cabinet pulls, and applied fresh paint, make a mental note of those observations as well.

Estate sale buyers are no different than homebuyers. They want to see photos of each room full of home furnishings, not just a general description. Homebuyers want to see more than the home's exterior. They all want to see sparkly kitchens and bathrooms, warm living areas and cozy bedrooms.

You can take photos with a smart phone, digital camera or camcorder, and upload them to advertising websites with instant mobile access. Your website should have photos with descriptions, upcoming estate sale calendar, details of the house for sale, map and contact information. If you already have a Real Estate website, it can easily be converted into a Real Estate/Estate Sale site. This will ensure that search engines locate and index any new information fast. Creating a website and getting it indexed takes 3 to 6 months if you work really hard. There are many websites and online tools that can help you advertise and promote estate sales and Real Estate.

Starting an estate sale business is the best creative way for a Realtor to sell household contents and the house to replace lost Real Estate income.

Insider Secret: When your Real Estate listings with photos, descriptions and contact information are posted on popular websites such as Zillow.com, an automatic back link is created to your Real Estate/Estate Sale website, which will forward potential buyers.

Finally, replacing lost Real Estate income with estate sales in addition to selling homes requires planning, patience and a lot of research. Managing both processes will give you the advantage of promoting your estate sales and real property in ways that very few competitors are doing to earn income. The more digital channels you use, the higher the likelihood of selling out estate sales—and selling more homes!

About The Author

You may know Tonza Borden as the Estate Sale Liquidator of *EstateSaleServiceAtlanta.com*, the highly respected and popular estate sale consulting and resource website. Over the last two years, she has built a very reputable following and has been featured by TagSellIt.com and interviewed by Columnist Michelle Passoff *My 2 Cents On Stuff*, EstateSales.org.

Borden has been helping people launch estate sales for many years; but the journey there wasn't easy…

Borden first had to work hard and learn how to make money herself before she decided to start teaching her insider secrets to others.

In 1998, she was striving to earn extra income for her family so she started learning about and **doing** estate sales part-time, which grew out of her hobby collecting and selling antiques and collectibles.

For one year from 1998-1999, she worked on her estate sale business daily while still holding a full-time job! She was extremely motivated to succeed. After years of perseverance and success, she **knows and practices these insider secrets—and she has not looked back!**

Since starting as an estate sale pioneer in 1998, Borden has come a long way in the "secret society" of estate liquidators and estate sale professionals. Today, apart from organizing 6-12 estate sales a year (by choice and design), she's a busy development executive for a non-profit organization, which is why she knows the sky is the limit for estate sales during boom or bust!

This ebook is in response to many inquiries about how to start a professional estate sale business, which is why she has provided educational materials to help you make an informed decision. It will not happen overnight, but it's easier (and faster) than you think. It's all revealed in this ebook! Remember, it took Borden over 14 years to bring you this information that you cannot get for free. Get in on the ground floor of estate sales and start benefiting from *Secret Of Estate Sales Marketing Success*. Now it's your turn.

Estate Sale Templates

Automated Systems With Estate Sale Insider Information And Exclusive, Professionally Formatted Templates:

- **New Client Package System:**

    1. Client Welcome Letter
    2. Estate sale Agreement/Contract
    3. Advertising Plan Sample
    4. Itemized Sales List
    5. Financial Accounting Summary
    6. General Service Conditions
    7. Frequently Asked Questions
    8. Consignment Form
    9. Testimonial Request Letter

- **Advertising System:**

    1. Advertising Plan With Major Estate sale Promoters
    2. Estate Sale Flyer
    3. Estate Sale Brochure
    4. Estate Sale Business Card
    5. Signs

- **Pricing System:**

    Quick Sale Price Recommendation Template (For Everyday Furniture/Household Items)

- **3 Special Bonus Reports With Valuable Information & Solutions**

Client Welcome Letter Sample/Template

[My Estate Sale Company]
["Your Unique Selling Proposition"]

[Date]

[Client's Name/Address]

Subject: [ ]

Dear [Jane Doe]:

We are pleased to welcome you as a new client of [My Estate Sale Company]. We feel honored that you have chosen us to fill your estate sale needs, and we are eager to be of service.

As you know, we are one of the few estate sale companies that provide professional, public and private estate dispersal for large homes. We guarantee a qualified team of experts, and a proven marketing strategy to turn your family's personal property into cash. We will do our very best to sell your own or deceased loved one's tangible assets in a dignified and caring manner. When you hire [My Estate Sale Company], you will get good value.

At the end of the sale, we will request a testimonial from you about our services. We are happy to be visiting with you to discuss your estate sale needs. Thank you again for choosing [My Estate Sale Company] to fill your estate sale needs. We look forward to a successful and profitable estate sale.

Sincerely,

[Your Name]
[Estate Sale Manager/Promoter]
[111 My Address]
[City, State 55555]
[Tel: (555) 555-5555]
[YourWebsite.com]

Estate Sale Agreement Sample/Template

ESTATE SALE COMPANY	CLIENT
My Estate Sale Company	Jim Doeman (Executor)
111 My Address	222 His Address
City, State 55555	City, State 55551
Tel: (555) 555-5555	Tel: (555) 555-5551
myemailaddress@uknowwhere.com	jdoeman@uknowwhere.com

This is an agreement to sell the [contents or partial contents] of the above listed home. The undersigned understand and agree to the following:

DEFINITIONS
1. "Client" includes legal owners, executors, trustees and administrator or other persons authorized by letters of administration to represent an estate.
2. "Seller" refers to the services hired by the Client, performed by [My Estate Sale Company]. Seller is responsible for all aspects that lead up to and result in the final sale and is entitled to a commission as defined by this contract.

SERVICES
[My Estate Sale Company] prepares for and conducts estate sales or liquidation sales, provide consulting services and/or consigning services in the manner agreed upon by Client and Seller. Services include promotional and marketing services, market knowledge, organizational skills, preparation and sorting at the date(s) and the place(s) and time(s) given.

CONDITIONS OWNER AGREES TO:
1. Client agrees that the Seller shall conduct this sale only, and that the Client does not have authority to conduct the sale after this contract is signed (_____).
2. Client agrees that no items shall be withdrawn from sale after advertising and/or pricing, sold or transferred prior to this sale (_____). If Client removes all "choice" items leaving only a number of ordinary items; these items by themselves will not generate the interest and crowds necessary to ensure that you sell most of your sale items.
3. Client agrees to show legal proof of executorship if this is the estate of a deceased person.
4. Client agrees to having good and merchantable title to, and the right to sell personal property on the named premises, that this personal property is free from all encumbrances, and that Client shall transfer and deliver such good and merchantable title to the buyers (_____).
5. Client agrees to provide suitable homeowners insurance against liability for personal injury or damage to the personal property or the premises on which that personal property is located. Client is responsible for these premises and their contents and will hold Seller harmless against all claims of personal injury or

property damage arising from or relating to the sale of the household items (_____).
6. Client agrees to hold Seller harmless for any breakage or damage although all reasonable care shall be exercised (_____).
7. Client agrees that Seller, in order to sell any item of this personal property, <u>has discretion to negotiate with buyers or reduce prices to the extent deemed necessary and prudent</u> by the Seller to consummate a sale. Any exceptions are to be expressed in writing by the Client (_____).
8. Client agree state sales tax shall be added to the price of each item and shall be deducted from gross sales (_____).
9. Client agrees to pay [$] for advertising and promotion, which shall be deducted from gross sales prior to total payable to Client at end of sale (_____).
10. Client agree for in-home estate sale conducted by Seller, the Client shall pay the Seller's commission rate of [%] on total items sold, which shall be firm and non-negotiable at the signing of this contract regardless of the results (_____).
11. Client agrees if the Client must terminate or cancel the estate sale during or after estate sale preparation, Client shall pay [$] to Seller for advertising and sale preparation expenses incurred (_____).

CONDITIONS SELLER AGREES TO:
1. Seller agrees to place all advertising for print and Internet promotion for the estate sale. (_____).
2. Seller agrees all items shall be priced according to liquidation value, taking into consideration, the area and what the present market will bear for a quick sale (_____).
3. Seller agrees to deliver to the Client, at end of sale, a final accounting of the sale. This accounting shall include gross sales, taxes, advertising, Seller's commission, rubbish removal, house cleaning, and total payable to Client in cash (_____).
4. Seller agrees to deliver to the Client, within [two (2) days] after sale, an itemized sales summary listing items sold for over [$10] with the asking price, sale price, and unsold annotations (_____).
5. Seller agrees if at any time the Client obstructs the Seller's attempts to conduct the efficient completion of the estate sale contracted, Seller shall terminate the agreement. In such circumstances, Client agrees to pay [$] to Seller for advertising and sale preparation expenses incurred (_____).
6. Seller does hereby agree to provide the services described above to [Clients Name], according to the terms and in return for the fee and charges stated above (_____).

CONDITIONS CLIENT AND SELLER AGREE TO:
1. This agreement and attached schedules contain all the terms we have agreed to (_____).
2. There are no other agreements, oral or written, between us. Any changes to this agreement must be made in writing and attached to this document (_____).

3. Any unsold items shall be:
   a. Donated to charity_____ (____).
   b. Returned to Client (____).
4. Removal of leftover furnishings and rubbish from the premises is the responsibility of:
   a. Client (____).
   b. Seller shall remove remaining furnishings and rubbish for [$], which shall be deducted from gross sales if required, labor and dumpster included (____).
5. Housecleaning of the premises is the responsibility of:
   a. Client (____).
   b. Seller shall provide thorough cleaning of [2-5] bedroom house, which includes bathrooms, appliances, cupboards/countertops, hardwood floors, all reachable windows inside, vacuum carpet, mop hardwood and tile floors for [$], which shall be deducted from gross sales if required, for up to a [5] bedroom home, supplies and [3]-person cleaning team included (____).

ACCESS:
Seller's estate sale agent shall have access to the above premises for the purposes of estate sale preparation on or after [Date].

DATE (S) OF SALE:
[Friday, June 29, Saturday, June 30, 2013.]

_____   _____
Seller [My Estate Sale Company]   Client/Executor/Trustee/PR

_____   _____
Date   Date

CORRESPONDENCE ADDRESS:
Jane Doe
My Estate Sale Company
111 My Address
City, State 55555
Tel: (555) 555-5555

ATTACHED SCHEDULE:
The following items are not to be sold:
   1.
   2.
   3.
   4.
   5.
The items listed below are not to be sold for less than the agreed minimum or "reserve" price:

Advertising Plan Sample/Template
Jim Doeman
222 His Address, City, State 55551

Public announcement of estate sale to newspapers and online publications include:

PROPOSED ADVERTISING   **ACTUAL COST**

Ad of estate sale to appear in the June-----2012 issue of the Community Newspaper serving more than 1 million readers, 475,000 suburban households in 11 counties each week, (insert Counties here)   **$45.00/2 Days (Fri/Sat)**

Ad of estate sale to appear in Thursday edition of Your County News, Paper #2, Paper #3, Paper #4 and website June-----2012   **$20.00**

Ad of estate sale/photos to appear June ----- 2012 on EstateSales.net serving (insert city and suburban areas)   ***$50.00**

Ad of estate sale to appear June ----- 2012 on EstateSales.org & Craigslist.com   ***$15.00**

Ad of estate sale/photos to appear June ----- 2012 in local major newspaper serving major city and suburban areas (Friday/Saturday)   **$15.00**

Ad of estate sale/photos to appear June ----- 2012 on Local-Deals.net   **$2.00**

Ad flyer of estate sale to appear [June ----- 2012 on Your Website. Notice will be sent to our mailing list buyers in the Atlanta and suburban areas.   **FREE**

Laminated outdoor signage at busy intersections in subdivision, staked in ground, located near the estate sale location   **$3.00**

TOTAL   **$150.00**

Note: Ads will run approximately one or two weeks in advance of sale in each publication to maximize results. The Client/Owner understands that he/she will pay for all advertising costs at the agreed budget limit of $150.00. *Per sale basis.

My Estate Sale Company   Owner
Date_____   Date_____

Estate Sale Flyer Sample/Template

Notice Of Estate Sale

Friday, May 20, 2011, 9am to 5pm
Saturday, May 21, 2011, 9am to 5pm
Sunday, May 22, 2011, 9am to 5pm

15 Johnston Drive
Anytown, MA 30199
Watch for Estate Sale Signs

QUALITY FURNITURE
COLLECTIBLES
CRUTCHFIELD STEREO EQUIPMENT, CHINA, SILVER TABLEWARE, HOUSEHOLD FURNITURE, APPLIANCES, FLY FISHING EQUIPMENT, FLAT SCREEN TV, SAMSUNG FRIG, WICKER FURNITURE, & MUCH MORE!

40-YEAR-OLD HOT WHEEL SET (100 CARS)

Estate Sale Organizer's Note: Please make plans to attend this super Estate Sale of quality home furnishings and collectibles.

TERMS:

- CASH ONLY
- Doors open at 9:00am sharp—Not Before
- Not responsible for accidents/lost or stolen items
- All items must be removed day of sale--No loading provided
- <u>ALL SALES FINAL</u>
- NO RETURNS, NO REFUNDS, NO EXCHANGES
- ALL ITEMS SOLD AS IS (BE SURE TO EXAMINE ALL ITEMS CAREFULLY)

My Estate Sale Company

Estate Sale Brochure Sample/Template

My Estate Sale Service

Need Help To Disperse A Deceased Estate? Need Help To Downsize A Large Home?

We Conduct Estate Sales of Entire Household Contents

Tel: (555) 555-5555
MyEstateSaleService.com

A hassle-free alternative to unprofessional methods

How much does this estate sale service cost?

Our commission fee is between 25-30%, minus expenses.

How do I decide between an auction or estate sale?

We provide on-site liquidation because buyers tend to pay more for items when they see them in their original setting. Valuable items such as period antiques, jewelry and fine art should be sent to auction for higher profits.

My Estate Sale Service
Jane Doe, Owner
janedoe@email.com

Don't make a hasty decision to have a garage sale until you contact us!

We will launch and manage your estate sale in a professional manner.

Services Include:

- Preparation, set-up, sorting, display and advertising
- Website photo preview
- Pricing
- "Broom Cleaning"
- Compassion and care

Call Today for A FREE Assessment

Tel: (555) 555-5555

Business Card Sample/Template

My Estate Sale Company

"We Conduct Estate Sales of Entire Household Contents"

Call Today for A **FREE** Consultation

Jane Doe
555-555-5555
janedoe@myemail.com
www.MyEstateSaleCompany.com

Estate Sale Directional Sign

ESTATE SALE

151 JONES DRIVE
Hartford Subdivision

FRIDAY, MAY 11
9 AM-5 PM

SATURDAY, MAY 12
9 AM-5 PM

→

CHECKOUT

BASEMENT

DOWNSTAIRS

PATIO

OUTDOORS
&
DOWNSTAIRS

GARAGE

NO EXIT

NOT

FOR SALE

MAKE

AN OFFER

25% OFF

50% OFF

Itemized Sales Summary Sample/Template
(Items Over $10)
Jim Doeman, Executor
June 29, 30 - July 1, 2013

	Asking Price	Selling Price	Item Not Sold/Notes
LIVINGROOM			

DININGROOM			
MASTER BEDROOM			
SECOND BEDROOM			
THIRD BEDROOM			

KITCHEN			
COLLECTIBLES			
MISCELLANEOUS			

JEWELRY			
SALES TOTAL:			

[My Estate Sale Company]

___Your Name_____Date_____

Final Accounting Summary Sample/Template

Client Name: _____
Date(s) of Sale: _____
Location: _____
Phone: _____

Gross Sales: _____

Minus Expenses Related to Sale

Minus Commission _____% _____
Minus Gross Sales_____
Plus Sales Tax 8%_____
Plus Advertising/Promotion_____
Plus Rubbish Removal_____
Plus Housecleaning_____
Total Expenses:_____
Total Payable To Seller_____

Total Payable To Owner_____
Payment Type_____
Payable To_____
Address_____
_____

_____
Client/Owner

_____
My Estate Sale Company

_____
Date

General Service Conditions Sample/Template

The service provided by [My Estate Sale Company] has been performed in accordance with professional industry standards. We have acted as an independent contractor. Our compensation was not contingent upon our conclusions of value. We assumed without independent verification, the accuracy of all data provided to us. Although it is not our regular practice, we reserve the right to use subcontractors. All files, work papers or documents developed during the course of the estate sale engagement are our property.

Our contracts/reports are to be used only for the purpose(s) for which they are stated herein, and no one may rely on the contract/reports for any other purpose. You may show our contract/reports in its entirety to those third parties who need to review the information contained therein. You agree to hold [My Estate Sale Company] harmless from any liability, including attorney's fees, damages or costs, which may result from any improper use or reliance by you or third parties. No reference to our name or our contract/reports, in whole or in part, in any document you prepare and/or distribute to third parties may be made without our prior written consent. We will maintain the confidentiality of all conversations, documents provided to us, and the contents of our contract/reports, subject to legal or administrative process or proceedings. These conditions can only be modified by written documents executed by both parties.

_____   _____
My Estate Sale Company   Owner

_____   _____
Date   Date

Frequently Asked Questions Sample/Template

Frequently asked questions (FAQs) may or may not be asked by potential clients seeking in-depth information about your estate sale company; but your FAQs will let clients query to get timely answers. Use this template as a worksheet to develop your own answers for tough questions during your first client consultation as well.

Why should I hire your estate sale company?

How much does this estate sale service cost?

We collect [25%] commission fee on total sales, which is nonnegotiable, plus [$150] for advertising and promotion costs.

Do I need an estate sale contract?

Yes. After we assess the home and you agree that an estate sale is the best choice, a contract is signed.

Do I need to know what I want to sell prior to the assessment?

Before we come to your home, we ask that you be certain of the larger and more valuable items you would like to sell. This enables us to make an accurate evaluation of your sale.

How long does it take to set up for a sale?

For effective advertising, we prefer three-week lead-time. However, the actual set up usually lasts 1-7 days. Estate sales take time, are a lot of work and sometimes messy.

How long does the actual estate sale last?

Sales take place on Friday and Saturday from 9am-5pm. For very large sales, we add a third day, Sunday. 80% of the saleable items are sold before 2PM on Saturday.

How can you ensure a large crowd for the sale?

First, the client should offer heirlooms and house wares that motivate buyers. Second, we use a number of proven advertising methods and various websites to advertise your sale with detail descriptions and pictures. On the first sale day, signs are posted directing traffic to your home. **Note:** If you remove "choice" items leaving only ordinary items, these items by themselves will not generate the interest and crowds necessary to ensure that you sell most of your sale items.

Do you allow friends or dealers in early?

We allow all buyers an equal chance for the most desirable items. We open your doors at 9am to everyone. If we advertise an item for sale it must be in the sale when the doors open.

Do you set low prices?

We try not to set too low a prices or unrealistic "high" prices either because we want everything sold. We work very hard to price even the smallest items in your house without making it seem like a garage sale. This ensures fewer disposals after the sale and more importantly larger gross sales. Buyers tend to pay more for items when they see them in their original setting.

How will I know what sold and for how much?

After the sale, the client receives an Itemized Sales List of sales over $10 within 2 days of the sale.

How will I get paid?

The client will receive cash or proceeds can be deposited into your bank if you live out of town.

Is there a minimum amount of personal property required for an estate sale?

A successful estate sale requires a certain amount of personal property to ensure a successful sale. A "house full" of original furnishings in each room is enough for an estate sale. We do not conduct "partial" sales for any reason.

What happens to personal property that does not sell?

Any remaining personal property is disposed of according to your wishes. We can donate it to a charity of your choice or [THE NAME OF YOUR CHARITY] [(ONE LINE MISSION STATEMENT)]. We do not have an agreement with a retailer or auctioneer to "buy" unsold items. We want it sold at the right price from your location.

There are some things I do not want to dispose of; can these items remain in the house during the sale?

Yes, however, we prefer that any items that you do not want to sell be removed or placed in a secured area out of sight to our team and buyers, as we will not be held responsible for them.

Do you remove hazardous materials?

We will not dispose of rubbish if it contains, or we think it might contain chemical, toxic, medical, radioactive or hazardous materials, i.e., paints, solvents, etc. We also do not dispose of pressurized containers of any kind or anything we suspect to be related to an unlawful activity.

Under what terms would you terminate service?

If at any time the client becomes abusive or obstructs our attempts to conduct the efficient completion of the estate sale contracted, we will terminate the agreement. In such circumstances, the client will pay us [$] for advertising expenses and sale preparation.

What if I change my mind and decide not to follow through with the estate sale?

If the sale must be cancelled, we will charge the client [$] for advertising expenses and sale preparation.

Where are your service areas?

We host estate sales in metro Atlanta, Georgia.

Do you have security?

We have someone keeping a watchful eye at all times. We will not hesitate to call the police for theft or disruptive behavior. For high-end estate sales, we provide state licensed security guards.

Does the client, estate executor or personal representative need to be present?

We do not recommend that the client be present. Buyers feel more comfortable negotiating prices when the client is not on-site and/or participating in the sale process.

We are moving and wish to dispose of some of our belongings, is this considered an estate sale?

The items you wish to dispose of belong to you or your family and are considered part of an estate. Estate sales are conducted for various reasons such as relocation, downsizing, change in lifestyle, debt, death, divorce, etc. **Note:** If you remove all "choice" items from your home leaving only ordinary items; these items by themselves will not generate the interest and crowds necessary to ensure that you sell most of your sale items. We do not conduct "partial" sales for any reason.

Consignment Form Sample/Template

Name of Consignor: _____
Address: _____
Consignor ID: _____
Date: _____   Phone: _____

Item Description	Tagged Price	Selling Price
Seller's Commission		
Gross Sales Total		

The following items are to be sold by consignment for a fee of _____% of the actual selling price unless otherwise noted. Advertising cost will be deducted prior to proceeds being paid to owner. [My Estate Sale Company] will not be responsible for any breakage or damage, although all reasonable care will be exercised. Thank you for using [My Estate Sale Company.]

_____   _____
Consignor's Signature   Consignee My Estate Sale Company

Testimonial Request Letter Email Sample/Template

[Your Estate Sale Company, LLC]
["Your Unique Selling Proposition"]

[Date]

[Client's Name/Address]

Subject: [ ]

Dear [Ms. Doe]:

Thanks for being a valued customer.

We'd love to hear how our estate sale service has helped you. Would you please take a few minutes to let us know what you liked best about [My Estate Sale Company?]

We'd love to feature it on our website.

Here's some ideas you can include in a written testimonial.

- What problems were you facing before hiring us?
- What did we do to solve those problems?
- What results did you see after using [My Estate Sale Company]?
- What was working with me like?
- How do you feel about the end result?

We're looking forward to hearing from you and adding your story to our [long] list of satisfied clients!

Thanks in advance for your time!

Sincerely,

Quick Sale Price List For Everyday Furniture & Household Items Sample/Template

Selling used and high-end furniture for a **"quick sale"** requires an understanding of the marketplace. Trends in decor, colors and styles can drop or raise the price of used furniture quickly. A high-dollar price tag on newly purchased upscale furniture can have little bearing on pricing the same furniture a year or more later, or during a bad economy (when the market is saturated with used goods for sale). Choosing a selling price requires pricing confidence that will draw the highest number of buyers possible. We use this legend to help determine condition (wear and tear) and price.

Legend:

Regular Condition=Up to $95
Quality Condition=$100-$200
Excellent Condition=$205-$400
Upscale=$405 up
Medium Density Fiberboard=MDF

VINTAGE/COLLECTIBLES

4 Dining Chairs (Quality)	$145
Roll Top Desk Oak (Quality)	$195
Vintage Dresser w/ Flip Top Mirror (Quality)	$145
1950s Dresser (Quality)	$145
Vintage 4-Chairs Dining Room Set (Regular)	$95
Vintage Cedar Lined Wardrobe (Quality)	$135
Antique Hurricane Lamp (Regular)	$95
Retro Rockers (Regular)	$35
Vintage Chest of Drawers (Regular/Quality)	$95/$145
Vintage Oak China Cabinet w/Glass Doors (Quality)	145
1940s Enamel Table with Built-In Leaves/Chair (Regular)	$95
1930s Walnut Chest of Drawers (Quality)	$135
Vintage Wardrobe (Quality)	$195

Vintage Bar Cabinet (Regular) — $45

Mahogany Duncan Phyfe Bow-Front Dresser (Quality) — $195

Vintage Trestle Table with Hidden Cup Holder (Regular) — $55

Vintage Console Table Oak (Quality) — $195

Vintage Shaker Sofa Table (Quality) — $105

BEDS/BEDROOM SETS

Twin Wicker Bedroom Set (Quality) — $105 w/o Mattress

Twin Bed Wooden (Regular) — $65 w/o Mattress / $165 w/Mattress

Single Bed Wooden (Quality) — $175 w/o Mattress / $195 w/Branded Mattress

Queen Bedroom Set Wooden (Regular) — $175 w/Mattress

5-PC Queen Bedroom Set Pine/Iron (Upscale) — $395 w/o Mattress / $745 w/Branded Mattress

5-PC Queen Bedroom Set Oak (Upscale) — $645 w/o Mattress / $945 w/Branded Mattress

Queen Bed Only Brass (Excellent) — $245 w/o Mattress / $545 w/Branded Mattress

3-PC King Bedroom Set Wooden (Regular) — $275 w/Mattress

5-PC King Bedroom Set Wooden (Upscale) — $745 w/o Mattress / $1145 w/Branded Mattress

King Bed Brass (Excellent) — $345 w/o Mattress / $645 w/Branded Mattress

BENCHES/TRUNKS

Cedar Chest Bench (Quality) — $125

Cedar Drawer Chest (Quality) — $125

CABINETS/BOOKSCASES

Country Hutch/Server Wooden (Quality)	$195
Wide 2-Shelf Bookcase Wooden (Regular)	$65
Curio/Pantry Cabinet Pine Standard (Regular)	$75
Corner Hutch Pine (Quality)	$145
2-Shelf Pine Cabinet w/Glass Doors (Regular)	$75
Custom-Made Oak Buffet/Server (Excellent)	$285
Display Cabinet with Glass Doors Tall/Wide (Regular)	$95
Credenza Wooden (Quality)	$125
Cosmetic Cabinet (Regular)	$45
Pie Cabinet (Quality)	$135
Cabinet Wooden (Quality)	$195
Dry Sink MDF (Regular)	$35
Entertainment Cabinet MDF (Quality)	$65
Four Drawer Cabinet (Quality)	$105
Country TV Cabinet (Regular)	$85
Four Shelves with Cabinet (Quality)	$105
Vegetable Bin Wooden (Regular)	$75
Tall Cupboard Wooden (Quality)	$285
Small Sideboard MDF (Regular)	$45
Small Hutch MDF (Regular)	$55
Curio Cabinet with Glass (Quality)	$115
Pine Dry Sink with Glass (Quality)	$115
Pine Bakers Rack (Regular)	$95

Bookshelf w/Glass Doors (Regular)	$95
Country Hutch Wooden (Excellent)	$265
Painted Storage Cupboard Wooden (Regular)	$75
Cabinet w/Design and Glass Shelving Wooden (Excellent)	$285
Small Glass Cabinet (Regular)	$65
One-Shelf Curio Shelf (Regular)	$15
Tall Bookcase Wooden (Quality)	$145
Glass Jewelry Cabinet (Quality)	$185
Painted Wire Door Cupboard (Quality)	$115
Small Cabinet MDF (Regular)	$45

CANDLEHOLDERS

Sterling Silver Candelabra (Quality)	$200

CHAIRS

Country Wooden Chair (Regular)	$15
Stuffed Chair Fabric (Regular)	$35
Wing Back Chair Fabric (Regular)	$35
Swivel Rocker Fabric (Regular)	$30
2 Club Chairs Fabric (Quality)	$145
Chair/Ottoman (Fabric) Regular	$75
Rattan Accent Chair (Regular)	$65
Rocker/Recliner (Regular)	$35
Bentwood Rocker (Regular)	$45
Executive Office Chair Fabric (Regular)	$55
LA-Z-Boy Rocker Recliner (Regular)	$95

LA-Z-Boy Double Recliner (Quality)	$245
Rocker Wood (Regular)	$45

CHILDREN'S FURNITURE

Child's Country Bench (Regular)	$55
Chair and Table (Quality)	$175
Child's Bench (Regular)	$45

CHEST OF DRAWERS

Chest of Drawers MDF (Regular)	$45
Chest of Drawers Wooden (Regular)	$75
Chest of Drawers Wooden (Quality)	$185
2-Drawer Bedside Chest Wooden (Regular)	$95

CHINA

Lenox (Excellent/Upscale)	$300/450

DINETTE SETS

3-PC Dining Set (Regular)	$55
Dining Table 4 Chairs Wooden (Regular)	$85
Dining Table 4 Chairs Wooden (Quality)	$145
Tile Top Pedestal Table/4 Windsor Chairs (Quality)	$165
Dining Table 6 Chairs MDF (Quality)	$75
Dining Table 6 Chairs Pine (Quality)	$195
Dining Table 6 Chairs Oak (Excellent)	$245
Glass Top Dining Table 4 Chairs (Regular)	$85
Glass Top Dining Table 4 Chairs (Quality)	$195
Glass Top Dining Table 6 Chairs (Excellent)	$245

LAMPS
Fancy Floor Lamp (Regular) — $55

MATTRESS SET
Single Mattress Set (Regular) — $65

Single Mattress Set (Branded) — $205

Queen Mattress Set (Regular) — $245

Queen Mattress Set (Branded) — $345

King Mattress Set (Regular) — $345

King Mattress Set (Branded) — $375

MIRRORS
Oak Mirror (Regular) — $35

Mirror with Drawer Wooden (Regular) — $55

Hall Tree/Coat Rack Mirror (Quality) — $175

Country Mirror Pine (Regular) — $65

MISC.
Bar Stool Oak (Regular) — $25

Plant Stand Oak (Regular) — $25

3 PC Wicker/Iron Set (Quality) — $195

Asian Screen/Room Divider (Quality) — $195

Bamboo Coffee Table (Regular) — $45

Grandfather Clock (Quality) — $195

Electric Fireplace with Logs (Regular) — $95

Dresser/Mirror (Regular) — $95

OUTDOOR FURNITURE

6-Piece Outdoor High Pub Set (Excellent)	$275
Spiral Staircase Plant Stand (Regular)	$45
Gold Iron/Glass Shelf Round (Regular)	$35

SOFAS/SOFA SETS

Sofa (Regular)	$85
Sofa (Quality)	$145
Sofa (Excellent)	$195
2-Piece Sectional (Excellent)	$245
Loveseat Fabric (Regular)	$35
Tapestry Loveseat Fabric (Regular)	$95
Loveseat Sofa Bed (Quality)	$125
Daybed w/o Mattress (Regular)	$85
Sofa/Chair Set Wooden (Regular)	$185
Sofa/Loveseat (Regular)	$195
Sofa/Loveseat (Quality)	$295
Sofa/Chair Set Fabric (Branded Excellent)	$355
Sofa/Chair Set Fabric (Branded Upscale)	$495
Sofa/Chair Set Leather (Excellent)	$345
Sofa/Chair Leather (Branded Upscale)	$495
Sofa Leather (Branded Upscale)	$1295
Queen Anne Sofa (Quality)	$145
Sleeper Sofa (Regular)	$65
Sleeper Sofa (Quality)	$105

Sleeper Sofa (Branded Quality)	$165

TABLES/DESKS

Office Desk Wooden (Regular)	$95
Roll Top Desk (Oak Veneer)	$f75
3 PC LR Table Set (Quality)	$145
Sofa Table Oak (Quality)	$195
Glass Top End Table (Regular)	$30
Queen Anne Sofa Table Oak (Regular)	$95
Computer Desk Oak (Quality)	$195
Small Roll Top Desk Wooden (Quality)	$145
Sofa Table Iron (Regular)	$85
1 Coffee and End Table (Regular)	$55
Lacquer Sofa Table (Regular)	$65
Painted Console Table (Regular)	$55
Accent Table (Regular)	$25
Mission End Table (Regular)	$65
Small Side Table Oak (Regular)	$45
Small Drop Leaf Table Oak (Regular)	$65
Butler Table Mahogany (Regular)	$75
End Table Iron/Glass (Regular)	$65
Desk with Shelf MDF (Regular)	$50
Desk with Shelf Large MDF (Regular)	$55
Small Side Table Wooden (Regular)	$65
Cocktail Table Wooden (Regular)	$85

Oak Desk (Excellent)	$245
Computer Table MDF (Regular)	$45
Computer Table with Glass (Regular)	$65
Coffee Table Glass Top (Regular)	$85
Coffee Table Wooden (Regular)	$65

TV CONSOLES

TV Console Wooden (Regular)	$85
TV Cabinet Wooden (Quality)	$125
TV Armoire Oak Large (Excellent)	$295

WARDROBES

Contemporary 5-Drawer Wardrobe (Quality)	$135

Supplemental

Assistant's Non-Disclosure/Non-Compete Agreement Sample/Template

I, _____ (Full Name), have been invited to assist [My Estate Sale Company] that has structured this sale and gathered information at considerable expense to them and their clients, and has been shared with me due to my possible involvement. I agree not to share or use this information, or use it for myself to enter into a competitive venture for a period of [ ] years in the city of [Anytown, WI].

[My Estate Sale Company] take this business very seriously; and we will not hesitate to enforce the terms of this agreement if violated. <u>We are not in the business of training or creating competitors.</u>

_____
Assistant (Print)

_____
Signature

_____
Date

_____
Estate Sale Manager

_____
Date

Rules for Assistants

DO NOT ask the staff members about sale procedures or merchandise.

DO NOT discuss the sale with anyone assisting the sale.

DO NOT discuss the sale with the buyers attending the sale.

Direct all questions to the Estate Sale Manager.

Be polite and respectful to EVERYONE!

Made in the USA
Monee, IL
05 December 2024